WIRIYAMU

ORBIS
BOOKS
MARYKNOLL NEW YORK

WIRIYAMU

My Lai in Mozambique

by *Adrian Hastings*

© Adrian Hastings, 1974

Library of Congress Catalog Card Number 74-76916

ISBN 0-88344-758-4

Manufactured in the United States of America

CONTENTS

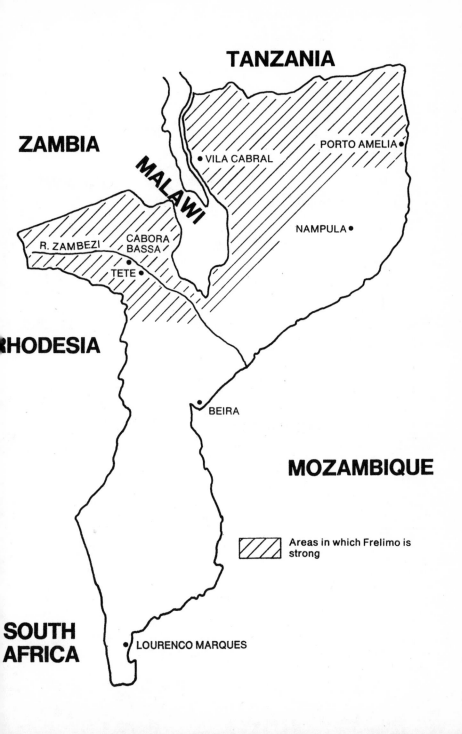

Introduction

THIS BOOK tells the story of Wiriyamu and spells out its lessons. It is not meant to be a general history of Mozambique, or of the wars that have raged in Portuguese Africa for the last ten years. But to be understood Wiriyamu requires a background and I have tried to fill that in, concentrating especially upon the involvement of the Church in the Mozambican situation.

The reasons for this concentration are clear: Catholic priests are in up-country Mozambique today almost the only group of people who can provide independent evidence as to what is going on. The reports of either side—the Portuguese government and Frelimo—are inevitably partisan. Journalists occasionally flit to and fro. What they see is often extremely limited. They never know the African languages and seldom know even Portuguese. Yet Catholic priests are not generally the most communicative of sources. We have to understand what has driven a considerable number of them to public protest. To understand this we must further examine the special relationship that has existed between the Portuguese State and the Catholic Church since the establishment of the Concordat in 1940 and the way the Portuguese government has understood the rôle of the missionary. Large sections of the relevant diplomatic and legal documents have as a consequence been included in an appendix. These documents have the most serious implications for the Church and I have attempted to set out what they are. It is not only because of the very oppressive character of Portuguese government but because of the Concordat that the Catholic Church in Mozambique today is rent in agony. Christians all over the world and of every Church need to grasp what is happening.

But Wiriyamu is not primarily a matter concerning the Church. The priests have in the end merely been witnesses and reporters of a vast human tragedy expressive of the conflict of colonialism with African nationalism and the desire for freedom. Wiriyamu is close by Cabora Bassa: the two names together aptly symbolize the whole struggle for southern Africa: not Portugal alone with its antiquated myth of imperial grandeur but Rhodesia, South Africa and the mighty world of international capitalism with its control of the most sophisticated technological know-how, are struggling today in the province of Tete. 'We prefer to defend South Africa on the banks of the Zambezi rather than on our own frontiers,' said a South African general recently. To defend a white-ruled southern Africa, to defend the dividends on South African investment, to defend Anglo-American and all that goes with it—it was in such a cause that the women and children of Wiriyamu were butchered. Let us not forget it.

A word about myself. I have lived in Africa nearly all the time from 1958 to 1971, in Uganda, Tanzania and Zambia, and have travelled up and down many other countries. I have written several books on Africa, the latest being a study of marriage problems in eastern, central and southern Africa commissioned by the Anglican archbishops of those countries. But I do not personally know Mozambique. I have never claimed to do so, but all that is written here is based on very carefully checked sources. I studied history at Oxford, and it is as a work of historical analysis that this book is written; though not analysis only: it is written also as a plea for a change of heart and for action.

In some ways the massacres are less significant than other aspects of the oppressive régime that go with them—the life of the controlled villages, the *aldeamentos,* and the continual use of torture. The three must be seen together.

This book could only be written because of the immense care in recording facts which has been shown by missionaries of the Burgos society and of several other groups in Tete province. To them I offer it in respect and gratitude, but beyond them I offer it as a memorial both of those who died at Wiriyamu and Chawola and of the few who survived. Finally it is offered to the new Mozambique, the Mozambique of the future and its leaders. Unlike the Mozambique of the present may it be a land of freedom, an African nation not a European appendage, and may it beyond all be a compassionate society—a land in which the little people be not trampled down.

Mozambique, past to present

Mozambique, past to present

THE PORTUGUESE was the first European empire to emerge in Africa and it will be the last to go. Guinea-Bissau, Angola and Mozambique, Portugal's three vast possessions in Africa today, are in some way the consequence of expeditions in the fifteenth and sixteenth centuries. The earliest settlements on the western coast date from the later fifteenth century. Bartholomew Dias rounded the Cape in 1488 and ten years later Vasco da Gama sailed on to India. The Portuguese Empire was under way. Forts were established on the east African coast at Sofala in 1505 and at Mocambique in 1507, and three years later the island of Goa on the west coast of India was captured by Albuquerque and quickly became the central point for this far-flung seaborne empire. Its wealth was in Asia but points on the east African coast were needed as links in the chain where ships could break their long journey to and from the east, and in Africa too profit could be found at least in slaves and ivory. A line of Portuguese fortresses emerged along the coast, each held by a tiny group of Portuguese, mulattos and native auxiliaries—slaves or others. Only in the Zambezi valley did they extend at all inland, establishing settlements at Sena and Tete, and huge farms called prazos, which developed as semi-independent principalities with their own slave armies; by the middle of the eighteenth century they were not greatly different from some other small African tribal chieftainships.

In the sixteenth century there had been a determined Catholic missionary effort, led by the Jesuit Fr Goncalo da Silveira, which penetrated to the inland African kingdom of Monomotapa in 1560. Fr Silveira baptized the king and many of his family, but suspicions developed and Silveira was strangled in his sleep. Subsequent missionary efforts had very little success. Priests, particularly Dominicans, came and went; the first generations in the late sixteenth and early seventeenth centuries worked hard to try to convert the local inhabitants to Christianity, but they had little lasting success—doubtless due in large part to their links with the warlike, slave-trading Portuguese colonists. As the years went on 'links' became simple identification. The Dominicans themselves held great tracts of land and dealt in slaves. Thus, Fr Pedro da Trindade, OP, who lived for many years on the Zambezi far above Tete until his death in 1751, traded in ivory and slaves, taught arts and crafts, and maintained his own private army.

What is important to realize is that Portuguese Mozambique through all those centuries was not in area the vast Mozambique of today, but a handful of coastal fortresses and a string of slave farms up the Zambezi.

By the mid-nineteenth century it had dwindled to a still smaller size, and missionary work was quite extinct. There were by then no more than three or four priests in all and Bartlet Frere in the eighteen-seventies wrote that of the few he encountered he could not 'learn that it was considered any part of their duty to attempt missionary work among Africans.'

Both Portuguese rule and Catholic missionary work have a very short history in most of Mozambique. Neither of them date from before the beginning of this century.

Mousinho de Albuquerque, one of the ablest of the men who worked in the country in the 1890s, described the situation with searing honesty in his book *Mocambique*: 'The administrative processes by which our colonies have been governed, or rather, disgraced, may be summed up as conventions and fictions. Vast territories conventionally ours where we exerted absolutely no influence; powerful chiefs tied to the Portuguese crown by fictitious vassalage; a system of government conventionally liberal in which improvised citizens elected in sham voting a fictitious deputy already designated by the minister, as unknown as he was uninstructed in the country he represented; conventional municipalities where there were no decently eligible town councillors . . . reserve officers without a reserve; battalions and companies without officers or soldiers; professors without schools and schools without pupils; missions without missionaries; priests without churches and churches without parishioners; even a medical service without doctors . . .'

With the European 'Scramble for Africa', Portugal, despite her great political weakness by the nineteenth century, was allotted very generous portions of the continent, because of her existing coastal presence, but it took a good many years, going well into the twentieth century, even to establish minimal rule over most of the inland areas she had so easily received. And after that establishment, there was little more to follow. The home country was itself too poor and too backward educationally to do much to develop its overseas colonies, and it was also in a state of great political instability.

The slave trade had provided the only considerable source of profit from Africa for Portugal in the past, and though theoretically abolished in the mid-nineteenth century, it in fact continued for many more years: Portuguese boats were still carrying off slaves from Mozambique in the 1890s. On the spot slavery was at last replaced by systems of forced and contract labour often not greatly different, and large sections of Mozambique were ruled by two commercial companies: the Nyassa Company controlled the whole northern part from its capital of Porto Amelia and much of the central part was ruled by the Mozambique Company from its headquarters in Beira. All this continued through the whole first quarter of the twentieth century.

Modern Portuguese colonial history starts from Salazar's *Estado Novo*, the New State, and the *Colonial Act* of 1930. Its name is significant. All subsequent policy has really flowed from the basic positions laid down at that time. The Act was, Salazar declared: 'A perfect expression of our national consciousness, and a close affirmation of the colonizing temperament of the Portuguese [designed] for the aggrandizement of Portugal . . . and to make clear to the rest of Europe our position as a great colonial power.' Such ideas were already becoming somewhat antiquated in the Europe of the nineteen-thirties but they could still be voiced elsewhere. What is unique to Portugal is that the assertions of that time, themselves derived from a mythological view of Portugal's previous history, are even today the inspiration of current policy. If slavery or forced labour has been one pillar of this policy, another of equal importance has been Portugalization: the impressing of the Portuguese language, culture and religion upon the peoples of the colonies—assimilation. For the fully-assimilated native there were to be no barriers; there was then to be no colour bar as such, only a bar based on identification or non-identification with the whole cause of Portugal. So backward in practice did the educational system of Portuguese Africa remain that even to this day only 3 or 4% of the population have mastered the first condition of this acceptance to citizenship — knowledge of the Portuguese language. But beyond that, how many Africans would ever wish to abandon their own cultural heritage and become in principle 'black Portuguese'? Even if they did want it, the opportunity was provided for a mere handful to be accepted in the legal class of the 'assimilado.' The 1950 census showed that of Mozambique's black population of 5,733,000 only 4,353 had been thus accepted.

If cultural assimilation has been one aspect of Portugalization, miscegenation has often been regarded as another. In fact interracial marriages are rare in modern Portuguese Africa, and mostly occur between whites and the 'mesticos' or already mixed population . But this latter group, unlike in Brazil, is not large—certainly in Mozambique not more than 1% of the population.

A fourth pillar has been the use of the Catholic Church. Article 14 of the 1930 *Colonial Act* speaks of 'the Portuguese Catholic missions overseas' as 'instruments of civilization and national influence.' Their work was to be done almost wholly through the Portuguese language, and both Protestant missionaries and non-Portuguese Catholic missionaries found it none too easy to enter. But the number of Portuguese Catholic priests and sisters able and willing to go to Africa was very limited indeed. Hence from a missionary point of view, just as from an economic or educational or political point of view, Portuguese Africa had become the most backward part of the whole continent.

From a Catholic ecclesiastical viewpoint, Mozambique in 1940 still consisted of a single diocese—Lourenco Marques. This illustrates how little missionary work was going on; to offer one comparison, the territory of Northern Rhodesia—now Zambia—next door was an area in which Catholic missionary work was decidedly slow in getting under way. It only really began in the twentieth century. It also has only half the population of Mozambique. Yet by 1940 it had already six different vicariates and prefectures.

It was doubtless to remedy this situation that the *Concordat* and *Missionary Agreement* were signed between Portugal and the Vatican on May 7, 1940. As there were so few Portuguese missionaries in existence, Rome was most anxious to be able to send many more of other nationalities to Angola and Mozambique. In return for this opening, it had to agree that all bishops and major ecclesiastical superiors should remain Portuguese, that the government should have a right of veto in their appointment, that (apart from religious instruction) church schools should use the Portuguese language instead of African languages, and that detailed reports of church work should be sent each year to the government. The government for its part would pay bishops the same salary as regional governors, would support missionary work financially. and provide free tickets for missionaries to and from Africa. In return for an increased right of entry and various privileges the Catholic Church was accepting bondage, the bondage inherent in being used as a deliberate instrument for the 'Portugalization' of millions of Africans.

The dominant and unifying policy behind everything which has happened from 1930 until today was seldom better expressed than in the following mystical words of Craveiro Lopes, President of Portugal, when he visited Mozambique in 1956. He was speaking at Beira :

'Here we are after more than four and a half centuries; here we are engaged today more than ever on a great and successful work, with the help of God, raising high the banner of Portugal, taming the wilderness, building towns and making them prosper, teaching, educating, and leading to a better life the rude mass of natives. disciplining their rudimentary instincts . . . moulding their soul in the superior form of Christianity, administering them justice with affectionate understanding . . . Everything indicates that we are on the verge of a new era, a decisive phase of History, of our History, that we have ahead of us a great, auspicious, and obtainable future . . . Everything is for the common good and aggrandizement of the mother country.'

✻   ✻   ✻

The Portuguese Empire continually lives in either the past or the future. President Lopes' vision of the future shows little sign of turning into the present. The reality brought by the nineteen-sixties was very different.

The greater part of the rest of colonial Africa was becoming politically independent. The Empires of Great Britain, France and Belgium were liquidated, and as this happened the inhabitants of Angola, Mozambique and Guinea Bissau became more and more impatient with the political status and general backwardness of their countries. Increasingly Portuguese Africa was being linked with South Africa and Rhodesia, lands ruled by white settlers. although in Portuguese Africa the white population was less than 3% of the whole. Moreover even less than in Portugal itself was any expression of public dissent or open political opposition tolerated by the government. The special political police, the PIDE (in Caetano's era renamed the DGS), took care of the potential opposition and as dissatisfaction grew so did the activities of the PIDE It is important to remember that the chief liberation movements —MPLA, PAIGC and FRELIMO—were in existence for some years before the wars began—as non-revolutionary political movements. Increasingly brutal repression drove them to open resistance, which began in Angola in 1961, in Guinea-Bissau in 1963, and in Mozambique in 1964. The violence of the régime had led at last to the counter-violence of the revolution and that in turn stimulated a still greater violence on the part of the government. The history of Portuguese Africa since then has been a history of war engulfing ever larger areas of the three territories.

While this book is mostly concerned with happenings in

Mozambique, it must always be remembered that quite as terrible things have taken place in Angola, where indeed in the initial revolt Africans, embittered by years of colonial brutality, turned in a fearful way to kill white settlers in their midst (perhaps two hundred in all) and were then the victims of far worse atrocities committed by the Portuguese. Of these atrocities the Baptist and other British and American missionaries tried hard to make the world aware, but with too little success—a *Daily Telegraph* journalist visited the area and reported that he had come across no evidence whatever to support the charges of the missionaries.

In response to the powerful threat from the liberation movements and the massive support they were receiving from the people in many areas, the government attempted not only to crush them by force but to win back Africans by an appearance of new policies. The separate native code of law was abolished and a new semi-autonomous status established for the overseas territories, and the number of non-white voters was greatly increased. But there is no evidence to suggest that these legal changes have brought any significant real change in the policies of the government or the white control of power or the general condition of the majority of Africans. Despite developments in the educational system the number of black people reaching university remains a mere handful. On the contrary, there is plenty of evidence that things overall have grown far worse these last ten years.

The war has brought about a vast increase in the size and power of the army and, even more dangerously, of the political police. Today the DGS is so powerful in Angola and Mozambique that it is very doubtful whether its actions are in any effective way accountable even to Caetano. There are liberal elements within Portuguese society today as in the past, in the universities and in the administration; there is a legal profession continuously anxious to assert the rule of law; and there are many people in the Church more and more unhappy with the drift of government: but these elements are next to powerless beside the DGS, the army leaders and, behind them, the big capitalists.

From 1930 until 1960 there was very little international investment in Portuguese Africa. Salazar was frightened of its effects.

In the last ten years that has changed. The Portuguese government has decided that it can best strengthen its hold on Africa by obtaining the backing of international capitalism. Today there is major investment from Germany, France, the USA and Britain in Angola and Mozambique, and the people involved in this investment are more and more involved too in the maintenance of Portuguese government. Hence a major new factor in the situation is that, whereas before 1960 Portugal stood much on its own in Africa, it is now involved in ever closer alliance both with the western economic world generally and with South Africa and Rhodesia. Despite differences of tradition, the governments of these three countries have discovered a basic unity of policy. All three are committed to the maintenance of white supremacy in lands which contain a large black majority.

Portuguese rule in Mozambique today combines then a number of things—1. an old colonial tradition, at times fairly liberal, more often pretty brutal, always very inefficient; 2. a mythological mystique of imperial grandeur resuscitated by Salazar and perpetuated in a somewhat muted form by Caetano; 3. a massive army with an increasingly powerful officers' corps; 4. a ruthless secret police; 5. a dependence upon international capitalism which has provided the vast funds for the Cabora Bassa dam project through organizations based on Johannesburg; 6. an ever-closer political and military alliance with South Africa and Rhodesia.

*　　*　　*

After the war began on September 25, 1964, it was for the first years largely confined to the north of Mozambique—the provinces of Cabo Delgado and Niassa. It is not the purpose of this book to outline the development of the war. Like all long sustained guerrilla wars, much of its course is extremely obscure. Time after time the Portuguese government has claimed overwhelming victory. and yet it has always become clear a little later that the war was still going on — indeed that Frelimo was advancing into new areas.

Undoubtedly the war brought misery to thousands of villagers in remote areas, most of whom were at least at first uncommitted to either side: the pattern of their lives in countless little hamlets throughout northern and western Mozambique was shattered. To isolate Frelimo and prevent the people from assisting it, either freely or from constraint, scores of thousands were compelled by the government to resettle in *aldeamentos,* controlled and fortified villages, far from the homes they had known, the fields they had tended, the little dams they had constructed.

'The rural hamlets are to the guerrillas what water is to fish': this is a constant maxim of the security forces. To get rid of the guerrillas the hamlets must be destroyed and the people 'removed' to *aldeamentos.* In most cases they are given a maximum of three days notice and at times only a few hours. Very few of their belongings are they able to take with them, and much that they try to take is broken on the way; even livestock has largely to be left behind. In their new settlement, very often surrounded by barbed wire, they are both 'protected' and controlled by the OPV, the African auxiliary troops, a group of thugs paid when the rest of the inhabitants are penniless. The popular name for such places is goat-pens (*thanga ya mbudzi*) and the inhabitants cannot even leave them for work without permission. Cut off from their old farms, which are then burnt down by the security forces, the people in the aldeamentos suffer immensely, especially in the first year. The death rate among little children and the old especially is very high. Conditions are all too comparable with those in the resettlement areas in South Africa described by Cosmas Desmond in *Discarded People.* Doubtless the material conditions will improve with time and some administrators will be more helpful than others. It may well be that some Mozambicans even come to prefer the stability that the controlled life of the *aldeamento* may finally bring with it, at least when this is compared with the perils of living in an old-type village which the army may decide at any time is really a camp of guerrillas. Yet the resistance of Africans to such settlements remains absolutely clear; if they go it is because they are compelled; but if they escape going, in an area where a number of *aldeamentos* have now been established, they may be classified as terrorists and wiped out accordingly. We have far too little published evidence from missionary sources about the way the war was conducted in the north, but Mgr Enrico Dia Nogueira, formerly bishop of Vila Cabral in northern Mozambique, and now bishop of Sa da Bandeira in Angola, has testified in court to major atrocities committed there by the Portuguese troops, and soldiers themselves have asserted that more terrible things were done in the north than have been done in the province of Tete. A Catholic missionary formerly there, the Belgian priest Fr Vic Nijs, has reported the burning alive of an entire village, and the English Anglican missionary priest, Fr John Paul, who worked in the north for twelve years, 1957-69, has reported many smaller brutalities.

In 1968 Frelimo opened a second major front in the province of Tete. This was in response to the plans to construct the Cabora Bassa dam, and Frelimo's initial object was to prevent that construction, in which it has failed. The power from Cabora Bassa will serve white South Africa principally and in doing so it will further tie South Africa to the Portuguese régime. Initially there was also a plan to settle up to one million white people in the Zambezi valley. It is clear that this plan is quite impracticable and has indeed been abandoned; but as far as the local people of Tete are concerned Cabora Bassa is a totally foreign project—even the labour employed is largely not Mozambican: it is safe to employ black Mozambicans in the mine compounds of Johannesburg; apparently it is less safe to employ them at Cabora Bassa. Much of the labour there has been imported from Rhodesia.

Though the spread of the war to Tete province has not held up Cabora Bassa, it has completely changed the province itself. Both Cabora Bassa and the town of Tete are now fortified encampments held in a hostile countryside. It is with what has been happening in that countryside since 1969 that most of the rest of this book will be concerned.

Not only in Tete and Cabo Delgado, however, but everywhere in Mozambique police repression has been growing worse in these years: more lengthy interrogations; more arbitrary arrests; more beatings; more complete disappearances. The political prisons have grown greatly in size. The more this process has gone on, the more unhappy many priests have become both with the political situation and with the Church's own official links with government. We must now look for a little at the first major protest from a group of priests. This group was the White Fathers.

One of the consequences of the 1940 Concordat was a big increase in the number of non-Portuguese Catholic missionaries admitted into the country. Missionary societies which had long worked elsewhere in Africa now came to Mozambique—the Verona Fathers and the Consolata Fathers (both mostly Italian), the White Fathers (very international) and the Burgos Fathers (Spaniards). These societies had methods of missionary work which had been developed elsewhere—they stressed the learning of the African languages, the development of schools at all levels, the training of an African clergy. It was really only with their arrival that serious Catholic missionary work began in Mozambique, that is to say well after the end of World War II. Their approach and methods were soon to produce tension with the colonial authorities.

Some of the Portuguese bishops warmly welcomed their arrival. In 1940 Beira was established as a separate diocese by the terms of the *Missionary Agreement* and Dom Sebastian Soares de Resende was appointed as its bishop. Without any doubt Dom Sebastian was the outstanding ecclesiastic in Mozambique for the next twenty-five years. Time after time, he vigorously criticised the injustices of the administration; he welcomed the White Fathers and other missionary societies and loyally supported them; he ran a newspaper, the *Diario de Mozambique,* the only reasonably free paper in the country; and he built up around him a group of Portuguese priests of like mind. He and his assistants were not concerned with Portugalization but with the service of their fellow men in the image of Christ. Yet in the clarity of his voice and the firmness of his action he was alone on the episcopal bench.

In January 1967 Dom Sebastian died. The troubles of the diocese of Beira have never since ceased. The first two nominations for a new bishop proposed by Rome were both vetoed by the Portuguese government, and the man who was finally appointed, Dom Manuel Fereira Cabral, proved an absolute disaster. His views were quite

opposed to those of his predecessor and he was also extremely
inefficient. Just over a year later a large group of his priests was
already petitioning for his resignation. He sold the newspaper the
Diario de Mozambique to its greatest enemies—a group of right-
wing white business people led by Jorge Jardim, an immensely
powerful Portuguese capitalist with close links with the DGS. Most
of the Portuguese priests who had gathered around Bishop Sebastian were now forced to leave the country and return to Portugal.
The White Fathers, for their part, found their position increasingly
difficult. Until now they had possessed the confidence of their
bishop; now they had it no more, and just at a time when the
government was becoming more oppressive than ever, and they
were themselves being frequently denounced for being pro-African.

More and more often their parishioners and even their catechists
were being arrested and tortured, carried off to prison and never
seen again; they were harassed for preaching anything about social
justice and the rights of workers or even for using an African
language for worship instead of Portuguese. All this, they felt,
could be borne with, if they had the support and understanding of
their bishop. But with Mgr Cabral and his colleagues they had not.
They found themselves as assistants, and in obedience, to a man
whose sympathies were impossibly different from their own. They
found themselves in fact victims of the Concordat system, tied as
ministers of the Church to the very régime whose actions were
oppressing the people and nullifying their own work. In such
circumstances they felt their very presence had become impossibly
ambiguous, while a deliberate and publicized departure would call
the world's attention to the gravity of the situation and the
Church's involvement within it. It is to be noted that most of
the White Fathers were working in Beira diocese and therefore
not in what was at that time a war zone. But a few were in the
diocese of Tete and their experience of what their parishioners
had to suffer was even more horrific. Their protest was not against
large-scale massacres which were not happening at that time in
their missions but against a deeply and continually oppressive
régime with which the Church had freely identified itself for a
mess of pottage. They were a group of nearly forty men in all—

Canadians, Germans, Italians, Spaniards, Belgians, an Austrian, a Dutchman and a Swiss. Their regional superior was an Italian, Fr Cesare Bertulli. By a very large majority they chose to withdraw but the final decision was made by the Superior General of the society, Theo Van Asten and his council in Rome. He explained it to the other members of the society in the following way:

'The situation of the White Fathers in Mozambique is in fact more and more marked by a grave ambiguity. Sent as they are to bear witness to the Gospel and make the Church present as sign and means of salvation, the missionaries find that the confusion between Church and State, which is sustained by the constant practice of both civic and religious authorities, does a great disservice to the presentation of the gospel Message and of the real face of the Church . . .

'We wanted, we asked and for a long time we waited for the hierarchy to take a definite stand to dispel these ambiguities in face of injustice and police brutality. Faced with a silence which we do not understand, we feel in conscience that we have not the right to be accounted the accomplices of an official support which the bishops in this way seem to give to a régime which shrewdly uses the Church to consolidate and perpetuate in Africa an anachronistic situation, which in the long run is a dead end. Deprived as we are of the means of getting things properly clarified on the spot, our presence only engenders a regrettable confusion in the minds of the people.'

When this decision was made public the Fathers were expelled from Mozambique by orders of the DGS at forty-eight hours' notice. The last ones left on May 30, 1971. The most senior Portuguese priest left in the diocese, Mgr Duarte de Almeida, was expelled at the same moment. He had been Bishop De Resende's right hand man and the editor of the *Diario de Mozambique*.

The carefully considered withdrawal of such an international body of men did draw the attention of the world and the Church to the state of affairs in Mozambique. A month later Bishop Cabral gave in his resignation. He was replaced after some months by a Goan bishop from Angola, Mgr Albino Ribeiro de Santana—

the first non-white bishop in Mozambique. Rome had at least succeeded in breaking the white monopoly within the episcopal hierarchy of Mozambique by his appointment. He arrived in February 1972. Hostility to his appointment, however, from white elements in Beira was intense. He was bitterly attacked and a bucket of human excrement was thrown at the door of his house. One year later, February 1973, he died of a heart attack—just after the military trial and sentencing of two of his Portuguese priest, Frs Sampaio and Mendes. Beira is again without a Bishop.

May 1971 to December 1972

May 1971 to December 1972

THE WITHDRAWAL of the White Fathers from Mozambique in May 1971 coincided with a very serious worsening of the situation in the province of Tete. The war was moving south and east as Frelimo continued to advance. Hitherto they had operated mostly north of the river Zambezi. Owing to the troubled state of affairs, the fleeing of villagers from the zone of operations and the burning of villages by the Portuguese army, the mission of Uncanha in the north west of the province towards the Zambian border had been closed already in August 1969. By 1971 far wider areas of the province were affected, in particular the district of Mucumbura on the Rhodesian border. We know so much about what happened in Mucumbura because of the quite exceptionally vigorous character of the two Spanish priests of the Burgos missionary society who were working there — Frs Alfonso Valverde and Martin Hernandez. But there is no reason to think that much the same thing was not happening in many other places.

We can best understand events by allowing these two priests to speak for themselves. They described at length what happened in their district between May and November 1971 in a series of reports which they sent to their superiors and circulated to colleagues in the hope that something would be done. These reports were later rolled into one. Fr Valverde has since testified on oath in considerable detail to the truth of these events in a Portuguese court in Beira in February 1973 at the trial of Frs Sampaio and Mendes, to which I shall return—and his testimony was not questioned. As they say towards the end of the document, writing in November 1971: 'This is the fourth report which we have personally taken to Tete.' In court Fr Valverde described that November visit to Tete in greater detail as we read in the trial's official transcript:

'With all these facts, Fr Martin and I wrote out a report without any commentary. I got onto my motor-bike and travelled 700 kilometres to Tete. We couldn't use the roads in Mozambique. These roads have been unusable for months because of the mines; we and all the shopkeepers in Mucumbura and the border and all those who wanted to go to Tete either drove through Rhodesia or flew. So I went on my bike, arrived and gave the report to the Bishop. He read it and was impressed. He even wept and said: "I am going to the governor immediately". "Bishop I also want to talk, I can't take any more. On the occasion of previous massacres I have always wanted to talk to him." "No," said the bishop, "you are very nervous, I will go and explain everything to the Governor."

'We were both interviewed by Governor Rocha Simoes. We gave him our report. The Bishop had spoken to the Governor on the previous day. He read the report and said: "Father, if you say these things happened I believe you, because we are having problems with the commandos here in the outskirts of Tete." And he told us some unpleasant facts which I don't have to repeat here.

"Governor," said I, "We are tired of pretty words. After the first massacre you knew perfectly well that it had been Sr Calado and Sr Trindade. Six months elapsed and it is true that four months later Sr Trindade was transferred, and now he goes on drinking and laughing in Chicoa. And Sr Calado used to earn a sub-lieutenant's salary but now he earns a captain's salary and commands a company of Special Groups (Grupos Especiais) in Mutarara. Governor, I can no longer believe pretty words." What the Governor said was: "Cool down, Father. I have nothing to do with the DGS, we are superior to agent Trindade. Sub-lieutenant Calado must answer for those events in Mucumbura in court." "But Governor, a man who kills or orders the killing in that arbitrary manner of nearly twenty people is now leading a Company of Special Group volunteers who, I have heard, are even worse than the commandos. I don't want to blame those men Calado and Trindade, who are small cogs in the machine. The big motors are much more to blame. And Governor, excuse me, I must say what I think. After four massacres I have had enough and I am convinced to tell the truth, that the most natural place for a Christian in these times is prison." "Cool down, Father, we'll see what we can do. I am also trying".

The priests had appealed to the governor. They had appealed to their bishop. They appealed to their brother priests. Thirty-six missionaries of the diocese of Tete had met together on July 1, 1971 to draw up a common line and urge the bishop to make a public protest against the ever more arbitrary behaviour of the security forces, but nothing was done. The missionaries worked far apart from one another while the central diocesan direction was not prepared to come out in public. At the end of November after his final fruitless visit to Tete, Fr Valverde drew up a desperate public appeal entitled *Mucumbura 1971 and the Rights of Man as recognized by Portugal in UNO*. Clear, precise, unambiguous, it published names, dates and the 28th Commando Company as responsible for the massacre of villagers. It was signed on November 28 by the two priests and the three sisters at Mucumbura. It was its circulation which provoked the priests' arrest—several copies were seized by the DGS from Fr Jesus Camba which had been intended for distribution at the Presbyteral Council in Tete on January 11, 1972. In the lengthy document of indictment comprising ninety-two paragraphs of charges subsequently formulated against them, paragraphs 70-90 are all directly related to this little paper; paragraph 71 relates that one copy was sent to the priests' superior in Madrid 'with the intention of getting it published in the foreign press'; the paper, it is said, makes 'libellous comments about our troops and our rulers' and accuses Portugal of racialism. Such charges warranted immediate arrest though twenty-two months later one was still awaiting their demonstration in court. A month after the publication of this paper, on January 2, Fs Valverde and Hernandez were seized by the Rhodesian police when they entered Rhodesia for a short holiday and handed over to the DGS. They were in Machava prison in Lourenco Marques from then until November 1973, during the second year in solitary confinement for 23 hours a day. At the end of it all they were released and deported under pretext of an amnesty to avoid the public trial they had claimed:

such a trial could only have vindicated the substantial accuracy of their accusations and would have been an extreme embarrassment for the government.

It is time to turn to their report.

MUCUMBURA 1971
BY ALFONSO VALVERDE AND MARTIN HERNANDEZ

AN AFRICAN chief (Buxo by name) was killed by men from Frelimo on April 27, 1971 because he was considered to be an accomplice of the Portuguese Government and a traitor to his people.[1] He had already been warned three times. On the same day a mine exploded near the river Mucumbura. Three Rhodesian soldiers were killed and two were badly wounded. The Frelimo guerrillas had set a mine between the two frontiers to keep Rhodesia from intervening in the war against Portugal.

Reprisals by the Portuguese Army followed. On May 4 troops rounded up some African workers, torturing them and forcing them to confess their relationships with Frelimo. The workers admitted that they had seen them once and one of them confessed that his own son had gone off with the guerrillas. They were kept in a wood as prisoners of the Army and on the following day one of them, after being tortured, admitted that he knew another man who had a nephew also with Frelimo.

The soldiers immediately went to this man's hut to interrogate him but, full of fear, he denied ever having seen the guerrillas. He was beaten and punished barbarously and after he was told that the others had accused him he admitted that his nephew had gone off with Frelimo. He was killed immediately by three shots in the head. The dead man, whose name was Aroni, was buried by the soldiers, but on the following day the dead man's three wives, with some men from the village, dug him up and took him to the family hut for funeral rites, as is the sacred custom among Africans.

While the body was in the hut there was a rumour that the

1. The father did protest to Frelimo about the murder of Buxo, 'killed in cold blood and in an arbitrary way.'

Portuguese soldiers were coming along the road to finish off all the people in the village. The three women left the body and fled into the jungle with all the other people from the village. We, the two fathers from the mission of Mucumbura, learnt three days later of everything that had happened, and we went to the deserted village to bury the body of Aroni, which was still in the hut in a bad state of decomposition.

On May 7, 1971, Portuguese soldiers, under the command of a sergeant and an agent of the Directorate-General of Security killed fourteen people. All of them were inoffensive African workers. They were beaten, tortured and massacred in the cruellest fashion, their only crime being that they had once given maize, corn and other food to the Frelimo guerillas.

The names of these workers who were killed were Guidibo, Miriamo, Grizi, Zeze, Kenias, Caropora, Fungurani, Pitroce, Maizi, Kenete, Matias, Diquissoni, Languisse and Jona. These men lived in Catacha and Kapinga villages which were in the area of our mission.

When we arrived there some days later we found no one. The villagers had all fled leaving their cows and goats unattended in the fields. The people from the neighbouring village, Mahanda, told us the names of the dead.

An eye-witness who managed to flee from the soldiers at three in the morning told us everything that had happened. He was obliged to dig the graves to bury the fourteen men. We saw one of the graves by the side of the river Dack. The man who went with us told us the names of the five or six African labourers who were buried together in that one grave.

He recognized their shirts and clothing which were lying about. The grave was shallow and as there were several people buried in it there was a strong smell of putrefying human flesh.

Some twenty feet from the grave we found a human head with hardly any flesh on the bones, ribs, legs and parts of the hands. The man from the village said that some of their companions had not been shot to death but beaten, tortured and cut up. He showed us big sticks thick with blood with which the victims must have been beaten.

This terrible supposition is confirmed by the following statement from an African 'bought' by the Portuguese soldiers to accompany them and to tell them the names of suspects. He said to some of our teachers: 'We killed a lot of people who were friendly to the terrorists in Mahanda and Kapinga. They didn't want to talk and the soldiers killed them with staves and axes. I also hit them on orders from the soldiers both with a stick and with an axe.'

The agent of the DGS wanted to cover up the massacre in every way possible and told us that they had not even been to the villages of Mahanda and Kapinga. However, we found close to the grave we mentioned a number of empty ration tins used by the Portuguese army.

On the same day, the Portuguese soldiers killed seven Africans in Mahanda, a village near Kapinga. The names are: Chimuchamo, Ringuinoti, Pensura, Wacheni, Joane, Gomo and Saimoni. It was the wife of Pensura who told us how the soldiers had gone through the huts and taken out these men to interrogate them and shoot them afterwards in the most arbitrary fashion. Another eye witness told us everything that had happened. He had helped to dig the graves and was set free as it was considered he knew nothing about what had happened as he had arrived just that day from Salisbury.

The next day (May 8), the same squad of soldiers on return to camp killed another four persons in the village of Antonio. One of those killed was the traditional African authority in the village. The bodies were not buried as the Portuguese troops had to flee from an ambush by Frelimo and the people of the village were too scared to go near the place.

On the following day, as it was Sunday, we went there to say Mass and we did not find a soul. Only after waiting a long time and looking around did we find a shepherd who spoke to us of the dead. We then returned to the mission to pick up some sheets in which we placed the bodies and buried them with the help of some of the men from the village who were beginning to return.

The names of the dead were: Januario (the village chief), Cheredzera, Kaswaswaira and Chirega. One of the dead had three bullet wounds in the head, another in the chest, a third had

his face completely blown in and the fourth had been disem-
bowelled. We will never forget that terrible scene.

We wish to point out that all the dead were African farm
labourers, peaceful villagers. Among them there was not a single
guerrilla. Some of the Africans who had been shot and massacred
were old men with grandchildren.

Those who fled from their huts to live in the jungle like wild
animals, full of fear and terror, are perfectly well aware of
everything that happened and could relate everything in full
detail: the places of the graves, the names of their dead companions, everything.

There are no secrets among the Africans. The smallest incident
is always related at night over the camp fire. This long, unhurried
conversation is the 'national sport' of the African peoples. We
invited to our mission in Mucumbura anyone who wanted to
come so that they could obtain proof and hear from the Africans
themselves about everything which we have written down.

In a conversation with Senhor Trindade, an agent of the
DGS, we informed him that the people from the villages were not
to be blamed even though they had given food to the guerrillas
as the Frelimo had been doing a lot of conversion work. The
villagers were completely unprotected by the Portuguese authorities who were afraid to go into the jungle to protect them. Who
had protected two African village chiefs killed by Frelimo as
they were considered to be spies for the Portuguese? We strongly
condemned the massacre of Mucumbura and told Senhor Trindade
that it was completely inhuman, cruel, barbarous and contrary to
the most fundamental rights of a human being.

He answered us: 'Terrorism must be fought with terrorism. A
cannon requires an anti-cannon. If you haven't got the stomach
to see these things, the best thing you can do is to go away from
Mucumbura. In a guerrilla war there is no justice. One killed in
time can save a lot of lives.

'You shouldn't meddle with politics. Your role is to preach
the gospel. I can guarantee you one thing: you will carry on
hearing complaints and cries from the Africans because that area
is heavily mined by Frelimo and our measures will be more

drastic each day.

'The human rights you are talking to me about which Portugal signed in the United Nations are just "books" (meaning things which are written down) and we are not here for any "books".'

The company captain in Mucumbura told us: 'Believe you me, I have heard nothing about what you are saying. Go and ask the DGS agent who interrogated the prisoners, but don't just defend the Africans. Think as well of the men of my company who were burnt to death by the terrorists' mines.'

We replied that injustice cannot be repaid by injustice (two wrongs do not make a right) and that the crime of a man who has been oppressed for years and centuries can find many more excuses than the crimes of the oppressor.

He turned the conversation aside saying: 'The villagers are to be blamed because they are to terrorism what water is to the fish.' We reached the conclusion that the Army intends to finish with the water (the villagers) so that the fish (the guerrillas) will die.

We have only talked about the massacre but we wish to make it perfectly clear that the treatment which the natives have received and are receiving in these interrogations is completely inhuman, as is being kept prisoner and being tortured in order to confess something concerning Frelimo. According to the DGS agent himself: 'The blacks only talk when you beat them.'

All the people of seven villages have fled either to the jungle or to Rhodesia. The crops, which have not been harvested are being eaten up by the oxen, goats and gazelles. The people flee empty-handed in order to save their lives. Two other villages on the other side of the mission have ceased to exist altogether. Their men were captured and taken away to the police office in Mague.

On June 7, 1971, a colonel, a member of the Mozambique court of justice, arrived in Mucumbura. He had been sent to clarify the position and requested a private interview with us to tell him everything that had happened. He came to us saying that he was one hundred per cent Christian and had studied Christianity.

Very few words are required to sum up the interview: 'If you Fathers only reached the scene of death the following day, I can no longer believe what you tell me. Your information comes from the blacks and by nature they are deceitful and full of lies. If you want me to tell you what I think, it is very possible that the terrorists themselves carried out the massacre on the night of Saturday to Sunday morning in order to put the blame afterwards on the Army in the eyes of the people.'

We could not tolerate this absurd comment and argued rapidly: 'Colonel, your statements go against the most elementary logic. How could Frelimo kill its own brothers in this manner if, as you told us a few minutes ago, the village has been giving them food and help for a long time?'

He replied coldly: 'Look, these wretches, they are no brothers. You know very well that there are still tribes of savages among the blacks. To harm us and to destroy the prestige of the Portuguese Army the terrorists are capable of anything.'

When we saw that the conversation was taking this turn, we understood there was no point in continuing to talk to him. We therefore considered it more convenient to invite the colonel to accompany us to the place of the massacre so that he could see with his own eyes everything which we had described.

Perhaps because he did not like that idea very much he left soon afterwards for Nampula, remembering to remind us that we should not waste our energy on police matters but that we should preach the Gospel in the manner of Christ who never meddled with politics. He also gave us many other lessons on the Gospel and classes on Christianity.

We immediately notified the bishop in Tete and the area governor of these things. They informed us that those who had carried out the massacre would be severely punished. We know the punishment: Senhor Calado, sub-lieutenant of that platoon, who was earning 12,000 pesetas a month, is now commanding a whole company and earning 25,000 pesetas a month. Nevertheless the governor continues to assure us that he is facing serious charges before a tribunal about which it is difficult to come to a conclusion. Senhor Trindade was promoted to the post of the DGS at Chicoa, a very much more important one than that of Mucumbura, as it is a centre for African political prisoners. There he can work without the hindrance of having any Father to make a charge against him or criticize his well-known methods of making his prisoners confess.

During the first fortnight of October 1971, the villages along the river Dack were the scene of much torture and many deaths of innocent lives caused by soldiers of the Portuguese Army.

The soldiers forced the people to stay in their huts and threatened they would kill anyone who tried to flee or anyone who was in the jungle. After this they started on interrogation, beatings, torture . . . everyone who was suspected received a terrible beating until he confessed something about the guerrillas. Those who did not speak were considered to be accomplices of Frelimo and shot in cold blood in front of the villagers.

In the village of Guvanseve they killed Damian Gonga, Asami, Chabwedzeka, Bikico and Tauseni. Damian Gonga had been a teacher in one of our schools for many years. The soldiers found on him a letter from one of the guerrillas and, as he did not wish to speak, four Portuguese soldiers started to beat him with the staves of threshing tools in the most terrible manner.

They called his wife and his two small children and started torturing him in front of them. The wife, who was pregnant with their third child, had a miscarriage and she told us some days later about the atrocities; they beat him with the staves from two in the afternoon until nearly four o'clock, when he died.

The woman could not stop crying while she spoke to us. We can also imagine the unforgettable impression which must be engraved on the minds of those two small children forever.

In the village of Kampemberumbe the following also died in the same fashion: Petro, Raice and Sami. In Karuvi the victims were: Waite, Macaju and Chasica.

In the village of Traquino, also known as Nyambidzo, the following were also shot: Mabanda, Tadeo, Lingirani, Bicausi, Tembo and Chamana. A woman called Majuana was burnt alive inside her hut because she could not walk. The soldiers burnt down all the huts in the village. They also burnt down the outhouses for the goats, pigs, and chickens, all the animals being eaten up by the flames. The first three villages mentioned form part of our mission. The township of Traquino belongs to the Estima mission.

As a result of these terrible events the following were taken as prisoners of the DGS in Chicoa and Mague after having been cruelly tortured: Benjamin (a teacher of our school in Dack), Linguitoni, Guidini, Kesissi, Andresoni, Bande, Kapemberumbe, Romeo, Chibunza, Baira and Masasa.

Among all the prisoners and dead only one had a son working with Frelimo. The only major crime of these men was that they may have given food once to the guerrillas. This state of affairs has no end in Dack. They continue rounding up men, giving out beatings and killing people.

What does the Church have to say about all this? The Church is not adopting any position, which is the same as being on the side of the oppressors, from whom we all receive money for our subsistence.

During the last days of August 1971, the men of Frelimo went to a village in Rhodesia on the frontier with Mozambique, to kidnap an African called Bauren. It seems that this man had been giving a lot of information to the Rhodesian Government on the Mozambique guerrillas. When the guerrillas arrived at Bauren's hut, he was not there and so they decided to take away some objects they found there to show him that they did not agree with his position as a man 'bought' by colonialism.

They did not burn his hut nor harm any of his family. Bauren notified the Rhodesian Government that Frelimo guerrillas had been into Rhodesia and immediately reprisals were taken.

On September 1 a big force from Rhodesia entered Mozambique and stayed for a week pursuing the guerrillas. All the villages they entered belonged to Mozambique and came under our mission in Mucumbura.

On September 3, in the village of Deveteve, the Rhodesian soldiers killed David, the son of George. It was evening and he was going out to look for his cows. As he was going along the path he was shot dead. The soldiers took him to a nearby hillock and left him there after cutting off his hands and feet. Three days later he was found and buried by people from the village of

Mandwe.

David was one of our best Christians in Mandwe and was married with four children. We arrived on the day of the funeral and went to meet the Rhodesian soldiers to obtain an explanation from them. They themselves recognized that it had been an error ('. . . a very unfortunate thing, Fathers. Sorry, we thought he was a terrorist'). But they did not go to David's family to ask forgiveness.

On September 5, a squad of Rhodesian troops arrived in the village of Singa. They took with them the three eldest children of Singa and told the old man he should not be scared and should go to where part of his family was hidden to bring them home.

Singa obeyed and went to look for his family. It was already night when they all came back, talking peacefully, along the path. But another Rhodesian squad shot them to death as soon as it saw them. Only two children managed to escape death.

The following died immediately : the chief Singa, his son Adamo (ten years old), his daughter Ronica, married a short time ago and pregnant, his three daughters-in-law, Matiguiri, Rotina and Ester. Also, two babies who were being transported by their mothers on their backs also died. One was the son of Matiguiri and the other of Ester.

When the soldiers realized what had happened, that they had killed a poor old man and a group of women and innocent children, they wanted to hide the atrocity. They made a human bonfire with all the bodies and burnt them. But a very strong fire is needed to get rid of all the traces.

There were remains of burnt flesh and the eight burnt skeletons which were discovered on the following day by the Africans in the village.

We arrived at the village of Singa a week later and found all the villagers so full of fear and terror that they had not dared even to bury the burnt bodies. The two children who managed to flee from the shots accompanied us to the place where their family had been killed.

Almost all the skeletons had been picked over by hyenas. We

took some photographs and handed the roll of film to the bishop.

Two days later the colonel of the district told us: 'Our Portuguese Government has heard that you took some photographs in Singa and has ordered you to hand over the roll.' We informed him that we had already given it to the bishop in Tete,.

We now know that the bishop had sent the film to be developed in Lourenco Marques and he fears he will never receive the photographs. The wife of Singa, a very old woman, could only say one thing to us: 'I am alone. I am alone.'

This old woman really has been left completely alone with eight children around her. These are the children of her daughters-in-law Matiguiri, Rotina and Ester. We did not know what to tell her when she showed us all these children who had no mother. The eldest is only ten years old.

Many witnesses told us that between September 1 and 7 helicopters landed in Mucumbura with dead and wounded. We cannot give further details because we do not know the number of the dead. They were buried quickly by Portuguese soldiers in Mucumbura. The Rhodesian soldiers were in villages a long way from the mission and we do not yet know everything which happened during that week of real terror in which the African villagers saw nothing but helicopters and armed men everywhere.

We are also aware that about twelve people have been taken to Rhodesia to be interrogated there.

On November 2, 1971, Colonel Craveiro Lopez arrived in Mucumbura. He called together the military and civil authorities and informed them of his plans: 'Within a very short time our aircraft and commandos will be all over the villages in the area of Buxo. Now is the time to burn and exterminate that area as we have given them time to get to the camp and not to ally themselves with the terrorists.'

A group of forty Portuguese commandos arrived in helicopters in the area of Buxo (some twenty kilometres from our mission) on November 3. They had orders to burn and exterminate everything they found and we all know that the commandos are always faithful and efficient in carrying out this type of order. They burnt all the houses and huts they found between the villages of

Mahanda and Antonio. We ourselves saw more than fifty huts burned. Among them were our school in Antonio and the house of the teacher.

Maize, clothing, chairs, bicycles, carts, everything was destroyed. We had gone on the previous day to notify everyone in the villages that they should flee as quickly as possible because we had heard that the Government was going to bomb them. Thanks to this the commandos found the villages empty, but not all.

On November 4, the commandos found a group of sixteen people when they were about to flee. They were all women and children. After questioning them about the guerrillas and receiving evasive replies, they forced them into a hut and started throwing grenades to burn them alive. All the women and children were burnt to death inside.

Only one woman, when the soldiers left the area, managed to flee from the burning hut. She had one shoulder completely open where it had been hit by a grenade. She told us everything and gave us the names of the women and children who had been murdered so barbarously: Helena (wife of the African chief in the village who had been killed by Frelimo as he was faithful to Portugal. Is it not absurd that the commandos should now kill his wife and children?) and her daughters Ester (10), Margreta (8), Maria (6) and Taferei (one month).

Of this family only two sons who were not with the mother are still alive. As they had nobody left we have brought them to our mission. The other victims were Majozi, a woman of sixty-five; Rute Chidekinde, a married woman, and, her children Kufa (ten), Massa (twelve), Veronica (eight), Rosa (six), Rebeca (four), and Maria (seven months); Dzudzay, a married woman (twenty); and Rorosi a two-year-old child.

On November 6 we went to bury them. The guerrillas arrived and helped us. We want to point out that the Portuguese soldiers during these last operations in Mucumbura, did not manage to kill a single guerrilla.

In another hut we found Haidi (an old man of seventy), and two other people who were quite unrecognizable, who had also been burnt in the same manner. Near Senhor Gabriel's shop in the village of Antonio we also buried another five people who could not be identified as we found only their burnt skeletons. Among them was a child of two or three years. We believe this was a family of an African of the Protestant sect of the Apostles, as we found a pendant which they normally wear.

The troops also killed and mutilated two African prisoners they had brought as guides as they had refused to take them to the guerrilla bases. These two were Julay and his nephew, who had been prisoners for several months and who were killed in the village of Antonio as they had not obeyed orders. The guerrillas look on them as national heroes.

Near Senhor Gabriel's shop, we found twenty oxen which had been shot. The animals were not burnt. And it would seem that it was an animal cemetery, a very dangerous point of infection for all the neighbouring villages. We do not know what the commandos did in other villages up to Mahanda. We can only say what we have seen with our own eyes in the village of Antonio.

This is the fourth report which we have personally taken to Tete. Truth will out. We have found an echo in our fellow missionaries throughout. But we have found no apostolic posture in the Church hierarchy or in the Government. We return once again deceived. How far will this go?

The Bishop of Tete, the bishops in Mozambique, all of whom know this because they have read our reports, and those from many other missions in the north of Mozambique who have witnessed the death of the innocent people and who are convinced that this is only the beginning of an unending chain of injustices, have they nothing to say in this historic moment in Mozambique?

Why have they been scared to talk about all this in the Synod? We have sent all these reports to all the dioceses and to the Archbishop at Lourenco Marques. Why do they continue gagging us?

But they will not succeed in this. We are grown men and can remove the gag and run all the risks involved in this. We must obey God before men.

We believe simply that we have a serious obligation, a very

serious one because of God's requirements as set down in the Gospels, to denounce and unmask the real villain of all these injustices. Those who are really responsible for the massacres and killings in Mucumbura are the political and military governors of Portugal who support and defend this totally unjust war.

The people of Mozambique, because of their language, culture, race, customs, mentality, philosophy, have complete right to full self-determination and independence. This is at the root of the problem which our bishop does not want to touch because he says this is "meddling in politics". This is a diabolical argument which the Portuguese Catholic governors like to use to continue invulnerable with their terrible injustices.

We missionaries in Mozambique have sinned infinitely more by omission than by action. Our neutrality during these decisive moments is really traitorous to the people of Mozambique. If we continue like this without treading on anyone's toes, we will lose for ever and we will be to blame in this crucial hour in the history of Mozambique.

Our bishops and we ourselves are protected by the government and we are hoping to receive more money from the state next January. Those who are persecuted, tortured, and assassinated are our Africans. Those massacred in Mucumbura were defenceless African labourers, women and children. No priest has suffered torture nor has he had to flee into the jungle to sleep night and day in the open with the tropical rains.

Christ was always with those who were down-trodden. And we, with whom do we run? We believe that, where Christ is, there the Church should be valiantly and clearly, with no possible ambiguity. In our opinion the White Fathers were very right in breaking with this terrible ambiguity.

From today onward we will take definite steps to support the oppressed, the guerrillas, those who despair because of the exploitation of those from above. No longer are we concerned about scandal of the bishops and the governors. We have only one concern: to avoid causing continued confusion and scandal to the little people, the disinherited, the guerrillas, the poor of Yahweh.

* * *

The next mission to the east of Mucumbura was that of Marara. It stands forty miles west of the town of Tete and some twenty south-east of Cabora Bassa. It was staffed by priests from a different society—Verona Fathers. Here too the same sort of thing was happening by the later part of 1971 as the war spread on south and east. By that time the government was trying to force all the population around Tete and even well south of the Zambezi into *aldeamentos*. Fifty miles to the south of Tete, around Changara, this was beginning to happen by September 1971 on the instructions of the GPZ (Gabinete del Plano del Zambeze). As the people resisted they were still more brutally treated: more and more arrests, more and more torture, more and more arbitrary shootings. It would be tedious to list them all, but the missionaries at each station watched this going on month after month. One of the Fathers at Marara was a Portuguese priest, Luis Afonso Da Costa, and it was he who was chosen by the presbyteral council of Tete diocese to make what was happening in Tete known to the world beyond. And so at Marara in May 1972 he composed the following document as a general assessment of the plight of the diocese and of Mozambique. It does, of course, draw on the reports of his neighbours at Mucumbura, in prison by the time Fr Da Costa was writing, but its importance lies both in its providing an on the spot assessment of a whole system of government and not only of massacres, and in coming from a Portuguese priest who is neither a White Father nor a Burgos Father. He too, of course, was quickly to be forced to leave the country, that very May 1972. He now works on a mission in Peru.

—Yet Another Year of Agony . . . With no Hope of a—
Resurrection
The Diocese of Tete, May 1971 — May 1972
by Luis Afonso Da Costa

ONE so often hears it said that the priest should not meddle with politics. His job is to preach the gospel of Jesus, who was never a politician. Those, however, who speak in this way can never have made a study of the trial that led up to the death of Christ. Among other accusations there was that of inciting a popular rising, of proclaiming himself Messiah-King, of stirring up the people . . . Thus it is clear that though Christ may not have been a politician, he was condemned from political motives. Is this not equivocal? The priest is involved in the political because, like Christ, he speaks as a prophet asserting with authority that no nation has been sent by God to impose its own culture on others; that no law may enslave a man and deprive him of his inalienable rights; that every man has the right to freedom of speech and to take an active part in public life; that every man has the right to be judged properly before being imprisoned and condemned; that torture can never be used.

Like Christ, the priest must be on the side of the oppressed, of those who cannot make their own voice heard. Like Christ, the messenger of the Gospel lives in full consciousness the drama of the lives of the people to whom God the Father has sent him. Now in Mozambique they have killed, tortured, persecuted, arrested people arbitrarily and they go on doing it all the time. Some have lost mother, sister, father, brother, friend . . . It is therefore the duty of the missionary to defend the weak, to proclaim their innocence and if need be, to pay the price of their blood with his own life.

I feel it to be my duty to expose publicly this face of Christ, broken and agonising, that is the Mozambique people, so that those responsible for the fate of this people may at last stop the massacres. I should like to be able to give to this Christ in agony some hope of resurrection, but I can't do it all alone. I count, therefore on the collaboration of all those who think of themselves as 'men of goodwill', and who see in every human being a brother who is Christ. The facts of which I shall speak concern only about one third of the district of Tete. Far worse things are happening elsewhere but I can't speak of them for lack of precise detail.

In the course of this account I shall deal in turn with massacres and killings, tortures and arbitrary arrests, internment villages (aldeamentos) and the destruction of villages, and I shall end with the attitude of the missionaries.

Massacres and killings

ON MAY 4, 1971 the Portuguese troops shot a certain Aroni of Mucumbura.

On May 7, 1971, fourteen peasants of Kapina and Catacha were killed by the Portuguese army. These are the names of the victims: Guidibo, Mariamo, Grizi, Zeze, Tapureta, Caropora, Fungurane, Pitroce, Maizi, Matias, Kenete, Diquissoni, Langisse and Jona. On the same day at Mahanda the soldiers killed Chimichamu, Ringuitoni, Joane, Pensura, Wacheni, Gomo, Sanhadadaza Saimoni. On May 8, 1971 the army massacred four people near M. Gabriel's shop, in the village of Antonio. The victims' names were Januario, Charedzera, Kaswaswira and Chirega.

In July 1971 the army assassinated a man called Therere at Estima. At the end of July 1971 two inhabitants of Chinhanda (Estima) called Augusto Fone Chirenje and Luciano Clement were killed at Chicoa.

On August 23, 1971 the OPV killed a man called Patricio at Maiyombe after having torn up all the identification papers that he had on him.

On August 26, 1971 the commandos killed a ten-year-old boy called Antonio Neti.

From September 3 to 9, 1971 the Rhodesian troops came to lend a strong hand to the Portuguese forces and massacred eighteen persons whose names were: Jacob Zensa (eighteen years), Sanfur Aroni (twelve), Paulo Zirise, twelve), David Jorge (father of a family), Pini, Singa (an old man), Ronica Singa (mother of a family and pregnant), Matiguiri, Terina and Ester (all mothers of families), also two babies, one being Ester's and the other Matiguiri's, a little girl of ten and two boys of between twelve and fourteen. Two corpses were not identified. The bodies of all these victims were burnt.

On September 9, 1971 the guerrillas killed the chief Chiundiza. On September 14, 1971 the commandos forced a fifteen-year-old boy, Sande Dausse, to act as guide. He lost his life when the guerrillas and the Portuguese troops clashed at Inhacamba.

On September 16, 1971 the guerrillas went as far as the alde-amento of Mfidzi and killed a man of the name of Ferrao Coelho.

On September 19, 1971 the Portuguese soldiers killed a certain Passagem Vinho, after having tortured him because he annoyed them by demanding the return of money that they had stolen from him.

On September 30, 1971 the army assassinated seven persons at Cambewe (Moatize-Tete): Chandiguera, aged sixty, Agostinho Chandiguera, Sozinho Chaguluka, aged twenty-five, Cinto Chandi-guera, Eduardo Chandiguera, all five being fathers of families, Kalua Siale, a cripple aged twenty-five. There was also an un-identified corpse. The soldiers didn't even interrogate their vic-tims. They simply shot them on sight.

At the end of September or the beginning of October 1971 the troops threw two grenades at Inhagalankope, killing two mothers of families, Mapalata and Dizieia.

On October 23, 1971 the soldiers killed three men working for Ermoque (the company engaged in constructing the Tete-Songo road) at the village of Inhamachola. Their names were Sinalo Tacho, Vunzani Sani and Manzissi Salamaia. All three were married and fathers of families.

On November 4, 1971 the commandos burnt sixteen people alive in the village of Antonio (Mucumbura). These are the names of the victims: Helena (widow of chief Buxo, killed by the Frelimo). Ester Helena Buxo, ten years old, Margarete Helena Buxo, eight years old, Maria Helena Buxo, six years old, Tarifei Helena Buxo, a baby one month old; Majozi, sixty-five years old, Rute, mother of a family, Kufa Rute Chidekunde, thirteen years old, Massa Rute Chidekunde, seven months old, Dzudzau, a young married woman of twenty, Rorosi, two years old, Haiti, seventy years old, as well as two other persons whom the mis-sionaries were unable to identify. Near M. Gabriel's shop could still be seen the half-burnt corpses of five other persons, completely unrecognizable. Amongst them one saw that of a child of between two and three years.

On November 12, 1971 M. Caldas, head of the OPV, killed a

certain Keni Dirao in cold blood at Inhacapiriri.

Just after December 15, 1971 the troops assassinated a woman of sixty of the name of Chaleka, wife of Gervasio Kairiga. It was done out of revenge because her husband had escaped from the prison of Estima.

On December 19, 1971 at Chacolo the commandos killed three people: Laeni Tikha, Saeni Alfai and Maki Godo, all three fathers of families.

On February 10, 1972 at Inhaticoma the soldiers killed a woman of the name of Kudeka Laisse. She was looking for her children who were hiding in the bush for fear of the army.

On March 6, 1972 the commandos killed another person, Gedece Telha. She was in the last days of her pregnancy. This crime was committed at Inhantondo.

On March 15, 1972 the soldiers beat up an old man of seventy so that he died. This happened at Antonio (Mucumbura).

On March 18, 1972, once again at Antonio, the soldiers killed Antonio Chinaca, fifty-eight years old, and Saeni, seventy-one years old. They were killed as they opened their stable door.

On March 20, 1972 the DGS (PIDE) of Mucumbura tortured to death a sixty-eight-year-old man called Macaza, an inhabitant of the village of Antonio.

On March 20, 1972 the army beat up a couple living in the village of Chumbandabue. The bodies of the victims were burned.

Why were these victims killed? What were their crimes?
If one were to look for an answer in the encyclical *Pacem in Terris* one could find it in n.27. 'From the natural law, established by God, springs the inalienable right of man to legal security and to his own well-determined sphere of law protected against all arbitrary accusations.'

If one tried to find a reply in the Universal Declaration of the Rights of Man one could read, in n.10: 'Every one has the completely equal right to see his cause tried, equitably and publicly, by an independent and impartial tribunal which shall decide as to the rights and obligations, or as to the grounds of any accusation having a penal significance which shall be brought before it.'

If one thought of looking for an answer in the Political Constitution of Portugal, one would read 'In Portugal capital punishment is abolished.'

But if one were really trying to find an answer to the question that has just been asked one would come to see that none exists on the moral plane. It is simply a matter of military strategy.

When a government bases itself entirely on force it sweeps away what we call the rights of man. The only object is to maintain its power and to eliminate all obstacles. Everything then becomes clear. Brutal strength must be flaunted, terror sown, in order that fear will prevent men from thinking of their rights or demanding them.

The people about whom we have been speaking were killed without trial. There were no witnesses, it was not known who had accused them. There was no lawyer to defend them. The only thing known about the victims is that they were killed. One is reduced to conjecturing; perhaps they fed some guerrillas, or perhaps they merely saw them, or perhaps a mine exploded near their home. Perhaps the Frelimo ambushed Portuguese troops somewhere in the area, or they may have had a son in the Frelimo, or they could have said that they had no knowledge of the movement . . . or they may merely have been weak—a baby or an invalid, someone incapable of any criminal act.

None of these victims were members of Frelimo. As far as we can find out the soldiers only killed two guerrillas, one at Mucumbura and the other (a half-caste) at Inhacamba (Marara). Now one has a better understanding of the communiques issued by the armed forces in Mozambique. Among the 'turras' (terrorists) killed were children, babies in arms, women, young girls, young boys—nothing but ordinary civilians.

Arbitrary arrests and tortures

'Is torture used in Mozambique?' If one puts this question to members of the DGS, or to soldiers or to the numerous agents of the administration, they deny it emphatically: 'How can you imagine such a thing! We hit them a bit, but you can't call that torture.' An inspector of the DGS gave me the same answer.

Concrete facts, however, force one to state positively that torture exists and is employed regularly in many parts of Mozambique.

Falling to the ground in a faint three times under the blows received, is that not, perhaps, being tortured? For that is what happened to a catechist of the Marara mission. Flogging with a strong stick and a whip until the hands and arms are covered with blood and the arm is broken; is that not torture? That is what happened to a certain Manuel Chawanda who was in the Tete hospital to be treated for such wounds. Where is a certain Driver of Inhamajanela who was imprisoned by the DGS at Tete and who has never been seen again? Why did they kill him? On September 17, 1971 forty men were whipped till they bled, is that not torture? To transform a man's back into an open wound with the blows of a whip, as happened to Chaoboka Chithando, aged sixty, is that not torture? To hit until the palms of the hand are one great gangrenous wound, as was done to Gouveia Chaola, an old man of seventy, is that not torture? Or to beat someone to death as the DGS did to a certain Macaza, aged sixty-eight, on March 20, 1972.

And if they were to let us into the prisons of the DGS, like that of Machava at Lourenco Marques, what shouldn't we see there? Meantime let us listen to Augusto Luis who was imprisoned at Estima:

They bent the fingers of the victim, tying the third joint to the second with plastic thread. The operation was carried out on all the fingers, one after the other.

'They forced the prisoners to sleep, tied one to another by the hands and feet.

'A rope was tied round the victim's neck and thrown over a beam. The rope was pulled slowly and when the torturer saw that the victim was almost strangled he let him sit for a time on a stick. Many fainted, others . . .

'A prisoner would be tied to a pole, arms outstretched; then each foot was tied and the victim was raised by the feet in such a way as to stretch the legs wide. This made it easier for the torturer to flog the prisoner with whip and stick.

'They beat till the blood spurted out.'

And the things which Augusto Luis did not see were even worse than those he saw. They did not want those prisoners who were likely to be released to see everything.

If the torturer, Chico of Chimadzi (Tete), told us one day how he used his brute strength in the DGS prisons of Tete, one would be able to paint an even more terrible picture of the torture used in the political prisons. If we could look inside them, how many castrated men, how many starved to death, how many inhuman things should we not see?

They beat men without any respect for the sacred rights that their Creator has bestowed on them.

If we wanted to write down the names of all those who have been tortured and those who are still being tortured in Mozambique we should need a great deal of paper! And if to the list of those tortured we added the names of those arbitrarily arrested, we should have enough to fill a fairly large book, the reading of which would certainly not please those responsible for the actual fate of Mozambique.

The explosion of a mine, an attack against the forces at once sets in motion a chain of reprisals. As they can't find those who committed the violence, and as, whatever happens, they must spread terror amongst the population they set about killing, torturing, arresting, violating . . . And what is their motive in all this? It is the only way to win. One misdeed is added to another, then comes a third . . . till the day when the whole people has been exterminated. The only ones left will be the mad ones.

In the face of this frightful situation we wish to raise our voices, crying out 'No one may be arbitrarily held, arrested or exiled' (Universal Declaration of the Rights of Man, art.9). 'No one may be subjected to torture, suffering or cruel treatment that is inhuman or degrading' (*Pacem in Terris*, n.11; Universal Declaration of the Rights of Man, art.5; Paul VI, public audience).

We stand against all this and we are ready to share the situation with our brothers who are being deprived of their rights. The only thing that counts is peace founded on justice and on the brotherly love that the Son of God has shared with us and has commanded us to have for our brothers. Nothing, not even death, could blot out the thirst for justice that floods our heart.

Internment villages and the destruction of villages
If one were to set about studying carefully the map of the following regions of Tete—Mucumbura, Marara, Chicoa, Zumbo, Chiuta, Chipera, one would find oneself facing an insoluble problem. One would ask oneself 'Where are these villages of Traquino, Chacolo, Inhamagondo, Chimandabue, Mahanda, Kapinga, Chitengo? They have all been consumed in flames. The army has made a total clearance. Even the animals have been wiped out. Quoting only the principal scores we can state that at Antonio twenty head of cattle were slaughtered by the troops, sixty-nine at Inhamagondo, seventy-eight at Zambeze, thirty at Mpada, thirty-eight at Deveteve, thirty-eight at Chimandabue . . . fifty goats slaughtered at the village of Inhamagondo, thirty-eight at Zambeze, six at Inhamachola . . . We are only speaking here of what we have seen, of what we have documented. All these animals were left to rot in their stables. To them must be added those eaten by the troops, two or three killed here, two or three there; without counting all the millet, the peanuts, the bicycles, the pigs and the hens thrown into the fire or looted.

One can get in this way a fairly correct view of what actually happened.

But what we can say about the internment villages? The first thing to do is to call them by their proper name; they are concentration camps.

They are surrounded by barbed wire. The internees need a written permit from the warders in order to go to work and so on. The authorities maintain that the 'aldeamentos' (internment villages) have been set up so as to protect the population from the attacks of the enemy. If this is so why was it that the 420 heads of families who were in the internment village of Mfidizi had to move out again? Simply because Ferrao Coelho, their chief, had been killed by the Frelimo! Why were the inhabitants of the internment village of Bandala the (chief) obliged to move out again into other villages? Once again, simply because the chief had been killed by the Frelimo guerrillas. And how many other villages are there, living in these same conditions? They force the people into an internment village to protect them from an enemy who isn't an enemy, but whom the government has made into an enemy. They are given no compensation for the destruction and loss of their possessions. The people are forced to change from one internment village to another according to the requirements of the military situation. Every one is made to go into these concentration camps because it is easier to control them there: that is the essential object of these so-called aldeamentos.

There is a paper with the title *Visit to Montepuez,* dated March 1969, describing the internment villages in the region and ordering all those in the Tete district to follow the same instructions. In chapter A, which describes the plan of the internment villages, we read: 'This one is rectangular, almost square, it stands on level ground. The number of straw huts varies between 200 and 300. There are some of 400 but experience has shown that it is better not to put up more than 250. This permits the maximum control of the inhabitants. All the straw huts are ranged in straight lines . . .'

The security of which the authorities talk and which one ought to find in the internment villages works out, in fact, in the following way: When the Frelimo attack the warders or soldiers of the village, when a mine explodes in it, when anything happens in the surrounding country, it is the people who stand the racket. It is always their fault, so ten, fifteen, twenty or even more are arrested and they are given a 'bonus' of protection: torture, prison, forced labour and worse still.

How can such injustices be reconciled with n. 13 first paragraph of the Universal Declaration of Human Rights (see also *Pacem in Terris,* n. 25)? How can it be reconciled with our mission as witnesses of the gospel? These are questions that cannot remain unanswered. And for us the first answer is to refuse to be silent. We cannot remain silent. We must denounce these evil things before the whole world so that governments and peoples become conscious of their duty to help this people to emerge from this inhuman situation, utterly degrading to man. Our only purpose is to contribute to the creation of a true peace founded on justice and brotherly love.

The attitude of the missionaries

Every one knows that the guerrilla war has been active in Mozambique since September 25, 1964. Ever since then several regions in north Mozambique have been and are all the time the theatre of military reprisals.

The question that we are asking ourselves is not, 'What was then and what is today the attitude of the missionaries and bishops of the dioceses of Porto-Amelia, Vila Cabral and Quelimane?' No, the problem upon which we want to reflect is the following: Certain missionaries of the diocese of Tete, seeing the heinous crimes committed here such as the mass killings, the destruction of villages, the torture, the political prisons and the rest, felt deeply that they must come together to think about the prophetic meaning of the departure of the White Fathers. They therefore asked the bishop to help them to have this meeting. It took place on July 1, 1971. Thirty-six missionaries, priests, brothers and sisters, signed the report of the meeting. One of the resolutions taken was that the bishop should make an official and public declaration taking a firm stand against the massacres, tortures and arbitrary arrests, condemning all these evil deeds as exceedingly grave offences against the fundamental rights of man. If this request was refused, the signatories of the report reserved the right to publish it themselves.

A diocesan presbyteral council was constituted on September 1, 1971. Those who took part in the meeting had complete confidence in this council and left to it the task of preparing the public declaration in such a way as to interpret the thoughts of all the presbyterium and not only of some. Time passed and the situation worsened considerably. The first massacre had been followed by four others. The killings and arbitrary arrests, the tortures followed each other in an ever-quickening rhythm as the guerrilla activity intensified. The missionaries put pressure on the presbyteral council and Fr Leonel Bettini resigned from the council in protest. He felt that he shared responsibility for the council's unjustifiable silence. The clergy had demanded that the local church of Tete should show her people that she was not compromising. But still the declaration was not made public. On January 15 of the following year a missionary sent a letter to the presbyteral council saying that he regretted the council's silence and to ask why it had deceived the hopes of an entire people. The bishop of the diocese refused to allow this letter to be distributed to the members of the council, perhaps because it would have forced them to examine their consciences and to take up a position compatible with the preaching of the gospel.

The declaration never appeared and the situation became even worse. This did not prevent some missionaries from continuing strongly to denounce the injustices. The government began to turn a very hostile eye on these persons. It saw them as undesirable individuals and the manhunt began. The DGS sent for the following and interrogated them:

Verona Fathers: Manuel dos Anjos Martins, Jose Villa Lobo, Luis Afonso da Costa, Leonel Bettini, Renato Rosanelli, Domingo Camano, Valentin Benigna.

Burgos Fathers: Vicente Berenguer, Mateus Carbonell, Martin Hernandez, Alfonso Valverde.

African diocesan priest: Domingos Ferrao.

Missionary Daughters of Calvary: Maria D. Vasquez Rodriguez, Maria Gaudenzia M. Talma, Maria Clemades Prada Rodriguez.

What crimes have these missionaries committed? The accusations brought against them are widely diverse: having defended a catechist who was being tortured; having translated into the indigenous language some sayings of the Pope or of the Bishops of Mozambique on the subject of torture; having started a Catholic movement for the young; having gone at night to pray with the people of a village; having made a tape of some stories; having started a study circle with the object of helping some of the more capable to continue their studies; having had the practical charity to give food to members of Frelimo who passed by the mission.

They went beyond the stage of mere interrogation. Two missionary priests were arrested, some were expelled, others had to leave the mission in which they were working because they were considered to be undesirable in that place.

Frs Alfonso Valverde and Martin Hernandez were arrested in Rhodesia on January 2, 1972. They had gone to spend a few days of holiday with some of their brethren who work in that country. They were forced onto a plane and sent to the DGS at the airport of Matundo (Tete). There they were immediately arrested and they are now in the Machava prison at Lourenco Marques. On April 20, 1972 Inspector Sabino called on the bishop, Mgr Felix Niza Ribeiro, at his episcopal palace, and told him that either he himself or the Religious Superiors of Fr Luis Afonso da Costa must get him to leave the country; otherwise he would be arrested. The reason for this decision was not disclosed. As things were at that time he was an undesirable person to have in Mozambique.

On March 26, 1972 Fr Henrique was sent for to the Administrative Office in Mucumbura. There Colonel Craveiro Lopes handed him an order coming from the Military High Command: 'It is forbidden for all missionary personnel to visit the regions to the east of Mucumbura during the current military operations and for an indefinite period. The military authority must be advised in advance of any journey to be made and will decide as to its expediency.' A similar order was handed to Fr Renato Rosanelli of the Estima mission forbidding him to move about in the region of Chicoa.

Recently Fr Henrique Fernando has been obliged to leave Mozambique on superior orders.

From all that has been said we can draw only one conclusion: In some areas the government considers the presence of missionaries undesirable. They are awkward witnesses.

Conclusion

We missionaries are for peace and against war.

We refuse to accept the state of war in which the country is being held. Therefore they persecute us. We are not allowed to write in order to enlighten public opinion as to this anachronistic situation of permanent injustice. Nevertheless we claim this right and we speak in the name of those who have no voice—the oppressed, the tortured, the massacred . . . We no longer believe in peaceful speeches which are not followed by peaceful deeds. We accuse the power that degrades the human lives of millions of our brothers. We cannot remain silent in the face of these unspeakable crimes. Because we are free men and wish to remain free, we cannot remain silent under the pretext that we are powerless to achieve anything in the present situation. Because we are free we speak frankly. The peace that we seek cannot be won by anything so unreliable as the senseless use of weapons that cost vast sums of money and can only kill and destroy.

Peace must be built by fighting the scourges of hunger, sickness, under-development, illiteracy, the political and economic slavery of our country. Millions have been spent since 1964 and are still being spent in a senseless war which has created hatred and has poisoned inter-racial relations. The laws that govern the lives of our people only serve the interests of the few, they are against the interests of the great majority of the people. The people of Mozambique don't know how to assert themselves. They cannot express themselves or develop as a people. Those who hold the reins of government uphold the economic power of the big capitalists and the military power of the army chiefs. Their rapacity has become a policy which aims at the destruction of the culture and the characteristics of this people.

In the face of this situation we missionaries feel that peace is not only necessary but that it is indispensable if man is to survive. Today those who desire peace must fight against the powerful ones of this world, against the institutions that dominate and the heads of those institutions; against riches and against a situation in which it is possible to have such an inhuman domination that it ends by draining away the resources of a nation and causing the death of so many human beings.

Our aim is to be able to give some slight but real hope to our people that they may one day enjoy full liberty of expression and be able to build a world that is not an accursed one: a world without war or famine or exploitation, a world where all are equal both by law and in fact, a world in which a man's nature may open out in full flower and he will not be rejected.

Marara, Tete   Luis Afonso Da Costa

That is the voice of a Portuguese priest who went out to Portuguese Africa in all honesty and zeal to engage in missionary work, who is far from being a political militant, and who is now in exile both from Mozambique and from Portugal, content to do the work of a parish priest in a remote corner of Peru.

*　　*　　*

The war in Tete province grew steadily hotter as 1972 went on. As Fr Da Costa points out, his own report covers only about one third of the province and is quite incomplete even for that. Even before he had completed it there had in fact been another major massacre—this time to the north of the Zambezi, between Tete and the Malawian border. Frelimo was very strong in the area and the main road from Tete up to Zobwe on the frontier had been frequently mined. In retaliation the army descended on two villages near the road on March 21 or 22, Ngunda and Ncena. The troops involved were two groups, one coming from Zobwe, the other from Capiri Janje, and some two hundred villagers were murdered in one day—a massacre far larger than any of those recorded over the preceding year in the Mucumbura area. The war and the terror that went with it were steadily escalating.

It is clear that both the bishop, Mgr Niza Ribeiro, and the governor, Rocha Simoes, had made protests of one sort and another at the increasing ruthlessness of the commandos and the DGS. They were now both removed. Mgr Niza Ribeiro was appointed bishop of Joao Belo in the more peaceful southern part of the country. In July Rocha Simoes was replaced by Colonel Armindo Videira of the Paratroops. He was to be both military commander and governor appointed to deal with the crisis situation that had developed, in which the security forces could beat up the villagers here and there easily enough but were proving quite incapable of hindering the advance of Frelimo and its increasing control of the countryside even in the very vicinity of the town of Tete.

These events were having their repercussions and parallels elsewhere. Next door in Rhodesia the journalist Peter Niesewand had at last heard reports of Rhodesian military involvement inside Mozambique and published news of it in November 1972 to the irritation of the Smith government. The reports were true indeed, but in fact over a year late: Rhodesian troops, as we know, had been operating inside Mozambique already in September 1971.

Despite the obstinate silence of the bishops in face of the Mucumbura massacres, full reports of which they had received, Fr Valverde's appeal late in 1971 had stirred up a number of hearts. Among them was that of a Portuguese diocesan priest, Fr Joaquim Sampaio, who was in charge of Macuti parish in the city of Beira, a man of 40. On January 1, 1972, World Peace Day, he preached a sermon to an almost entirely white middle-class congregation at the evening Mass on the theme, 'If you desire peace, work for justice', and towards the end of the sermon he spoke of the recent massacres, the previous November, in Mucumbura. He offered them as one very clear example of the current state of injustice prevailing in Mozambique. 'We do nothing', he concluded, 'We do not protest at this barbarity— some because of fear, others because of their economic interest in allowing this slaughter to continue.'

A few days later he, his curate, Fr Fernando Mendes, and an African mission servant were all arrested on various charges. Fr Mendes had on one occasion refused to allow a Scout Troop to bring the Portuguese flag into church because of its connection for many Mozambicans with 'colonialism, exploitation and domination'. After over a year of imprisonment the two priests were brought to trial in January 1973 in Beira, accused of attempting to separate Portuguese territory from the Motherland. The trial was an interesting one, both because of the care of the judges in assessing the accusations very precisely and of the weight of evidence brought in defence to show that the two priests had been doing their priestly duty in a reasonable manner. Among the witnesses for the defence were several bishops and Fr Valverde who was brought from Machava prison to authenticate the massacres which Fr Sampaio had referred to in his sermon. The judge accepted the evidence but held that the preacher had still been wrongly 'carried away' by the vehemence of his feelings. The two men were found guilty of relatively minor offences. Sampaio was given a twenty months suspended sentence and Mendes a five months sentence, which had already been more than served while waiting for the trial. They were both returned to Portugal, where the case has never been reported in the newspapers.

The vicar general of the Beira diocese at the time was Fr José De Souza, a Jesuit. He too gave evidence at the trial. Five years ago, he said, twenty-four priests in the diocese had asked for the authority to speak out from the pulpit against the evils they encountered. Of the twenty-four all except Fr Sampaio had already been sent back to Portugal by government order 'and Fr Sampaio stands accused by this court today. Who is the right authority to judge priests who speak the truth from the pulpit? Is it to be the bishops or the DGS? What we have here is a scandalous society.'

Infinitely more serious than the arrest of Peter Niesewand in Salisbury or Frs Sampaio and Mendes in Beira was that of at least two hundred leaders of the Protestant Churches in southern Mozambique in and after June 1972. They included Presbyterians, Congregationalists, Wesleyans, Adventists and Pentecostals. Unlike Sampaio and Mendes these men were black and could not count on the consideration and final careful trial that the Portuguese priests received. Their arrest was not linked with the happenings in Tete, nor is the war waging at present around Lourenco Marques which is where the Presbyterian Church, for instance is to be found. But the DGS is at work everywhere and found it desirable to place the chief pastors and lay leaders of the Protestant Churches, but not the Anglican Church, in Machava detention camp to join the very many hundreds of black political detainees already there.

Whom did these arrests include? Let us look at one Church— the Presbyterian. They included Pastor Zedequias Manganhela, the president of the synodal council. A married man of sixty, he was well known abroad and greatly respected, particularly in the Swiss Presbyterian Church, for his faith and great sense of responsibility in the leadership of his Church. With him was arrested Pastor Casimir Matie, the vice-president of the synodal council, a man of sixty-four; Pastor Gabriel Macavi, former president of the synodal council, aged seventy-five; Pastor Abrao Aldasse of the parish of Covo in Lourenco Marques, aged sixty-seven, and with them many other pastors, evangelists and lay leaders. Are these likely political conspirators? If they are thought so, must not the régime which could conceivably drive a group of elderly and undoubtedly conservative pastors to sedition be truly a terrible one?

After arrest they were constantly interrogated and maltreated; some of the group were fearfully beaten both on the hands and on the back. Then on the night of December 10-11, Zedequias Manganhela was found hanged in his prison cell. He had been interrogated for months by Senhor Lontrao, a senior DGS inspector who, previous to 1969, had acquired a terrible reputation in Vila Cabral in the north, where he was only too well known to Anglicans in the area; more recently in Beira he featured in the White Father dossier: Father Bertulli gives an instance of brutality under the 'reign' of this man: 'A police agent (a white man) attacked a young man, beating him over the head with a stick. He split his skull. Maddened by the screams of the poor boy "he finished him off" ' (The Guardian, August 3). It was Lontrao who was now personally responsible for the interrogation of Pastor Manganhela.

Even in the long history of Portuguese ill-treatment of the Protestant Churches, this event stands out in shame. It was announced that he had killed himself, and that—as so often in colonial history—was intended to be the end of it. Doubtless there are many, all too many, less distinguished Africans whose deaths in Machava pass un-noticed. But in this case international pressure was brought to bear on Lisbon, particularly from Switzerland, and a secret inquiry was ordered to be held. It was carried out by the respected President of the Court of Appeals in Lourenco Marques, Valadas Preto. This judge confirmed on April 12 that Manganhela had indeed committed suicide but only after consistent torture, part of the common treatment of inmates of Machava. He was dismissed a week later. Twenty-four lawyers

in Lourenco Marques thereupon signed a telegram of protest to
Caetano and as a consequence the judge was reinstated. No news
of these events was, of course, published and Preto's report about
the treatment of prisoners at Machava was entirely suppressed.

Manganhela was not the only one of the Protestant leaders to
die in Machava. On December 19 the authorities announced that
yet another had killed himself—José Siduvo, and that he had done
so five months before, on July 21. The delay in passing on the
news was not explained. On December 24 most of the rest, some
of whom had received over a hundred strokes of the whip at one
time when under interrogation they denied using the church as
a cover for Frelimo, were released. Many took months to recover.
A full account of these events has been put together by Niall
MacDermot, the Secretary-General of the International Commission
of Jurists. It throws the most terrible light upon the government
that Caetano presides over, revealing as it does not some sudden
explosion of the military but the regular treatment over the months
by the political police of a group of distinguished African citizens.
Yet did the Presbyterian Church of Scotland raise its voice in
horror when the British government only a few months later
entertained the men who pay for and authorize such barbarities?
What did it say to Sir Alec Douglas Home? What did the Church
of England say, having recently appointed a Portuguese nationalist Anglican bishop in Mozambique, about the torture of Protestant pastors? Where is the Christian voice in Britain today? Are
only Spanish priests left to protest?

Whether pastor Manganhela did in fact kill himself after pro-
longed torture or whether he was not only tortured but also
killed by the DGS, we shall probably never know. Either way
his death stands out to denounce the monstrous oppression that
is now raging in Mozambique, an oppression carried on above all
by the omnipresent political police, the DGS, despite other elements in the Portuguese system, notably the lawyers, who are still
struggling for a modicum of justice. Yet, terrible as the death of
Zedequias Manganhela was, a still more appalling event was to
take place only five days later.

December 16, 1972

December 16, 1972

THE TOWN of Tete stands on the Zambezi some sixty miles down stream from Cabora Bassa. About fifteen miles further down, the Zambezi is joined on the southern side by the Luenha or Ruenya. This river and the Mazoe which merges with it twenty miles to the west flow north east into the Zambezi valley bringing water from the eastern highlands of Rhodesia. The Zambezi and the Luenha form two sides of a small triangle south of Tete, the third western side being constituted by the Tete-Beira road which runs south out of the town towards Changara. Up to the end of 1972 this triangle was—on African standards—fairly thickly populated with villages, hamlets and individual settlements, many of whose inhabitants worked in the town of Tete.

It appears that about December 14 a small Portuguese aircraft flying from Beira to Tete was fired at over this area and hit. It landed safely but its occupants, including a certain Senhor Jorge Guera, complained to the DGS in Tete and then to the army. It was decided that the shot had been fired from an area which included the villages of Wiriyamu, Chawola and Juwau. On December 15 Chico Kachavi, a black DGS agent of great strength well-known and much feared as a torturer in Tete prison, was sent to make enquiries of the local inhabitants about the presence of Frelimo. It was he who in April 1971 had, together with a white inspector, grievously beaten a Catholic catechist of Marara, Xavier Tomas, who only escaped with his life owing to the rapid intervention of several missionaries. He now visited Wiriyamu and other places but, not surprisingly, elicited no information. An army patrol was then sent to investigate but was ambushed by some Frelimo men near Corneta, a village on the Beira-Tete road. The soldiers set about burning the huts in Corneta but their inhabitants had already fled away from the road.

It was apparently decided to teach the people a lesson by carrying out a major reprisal. It took place on the afternoon of December 16 and began when some, doubtless small, bombs were dropped from a plane on Wiriyamu, probably the largest village in the area. Soon afterwards black and white troops of the 6th Commando Group arrived in helicopters, surrounded Wiriyamu and entered it. The people were lined up, men in one group, women in another. For the most part they were then shot, but others were herded into houses which were set on fire, while some of the children were kicked to death and other individuals were murdered in various atrocious ways. While the work was done by a group of soldiers, both black and white, and white army officers were present, some of the orders were given by DGS agents. Chico Kachavi, in particular, was back again, and he kept on yelling 'Kill them all. These are the orders of our chief.'

The massacre at Wiriyamu took some time. Following it, the troops turned on other villages and hamlets round about. As to what happened in some places we have no reports—only bodies were found; but in the village of Chawola, where they seem to have arrived last and time was probably running out, the people were simply lined up in a single group, told to clap their hands, and shot. The bodies were gathered together, covered with straw and set alight. In this rather hasty operation several people were only wounded and managed to get away. The troops then returned to Tete.

This summary account of events is pieced together, not only from the two reports which were written shortly afterwards but from later investigations of which four in particular may be noted here: that of the *Sunday Times* reporter Peter Pringle (*Sunday Times*, August 5); that of the Italian journalist Antonio Filippini whose report and photographs were published in the Milanese *Famiglia Cristiana* for September 16; that of the Johannesburg *Star*, based on Portuguese sources and published September 25; that of Frelimo, published in *Mozambique Revolution*, Dar es Salaam, no. 56.

Just south of the town of Tete lies the mission of San Pedro, run by two Spanish priests of the Burgos society, the one African priest in the diocese, Fr Domingos Ferrao, and a number of sisters working in the hospital. Some of those who escaped wounded from Chawola soon made for the San Pedro hospital. But the news was spread around not only by those who had escaped immediate death. There were many other people in the area who had seen the arrival of the plane and the helicopters and the light from the burning huts. There were refugees fleeing in all directions —some trying to get to the comparative protection of the town of Tete, others on the contrary thinking it safer to move away south. Fr Vicente Berenguer was travelling by bus into Tete the next day, Sunday the 17th, from Changara, and the first definite news of what had happened to reach the mission may well have come from him.

The bus stopped about ten or eleven miles from Tete, in the neighbourhood of Wiriyamu: 'There was a large group of people on the road, mostly women and children, carrying all kinds of belongings. Some were half naked. All were excited and distressed. The bus stopped for a long time. There was a discussion because the driver wanted them to pay.

'Eventually some of them came on board. They told me and others on the bus of great destruction in their area. They spoke of many missing relatives.

'It was not only Wiriyamu which suffered,. That is why there were so many refugees. Wiriyamu . . . is a village which, like others there, is somewhat dispersed. It is part of the regulo (a territorial division) called Gandali . . . This regulo includes other villages besides Wiriyamu and some suffered in the same attack. Several thousand people live in this regulo.

'When the bus arrived in Tete, another crowd of refugees was waiting. There was a lot of excitement, with everybody asking everybody else about missing relatives or friends. Many people were crying. And before we reached Tete, I saw many burned huts by the roadside. But the massacre did not take place there next to the road. Most people living there escaped.' (*The Times*, July 18).

The news was soon spreading all over Tete. The military themselves were not all going to keep it secret, and there were numerous witnesses at a distance, people like the man who said: 'I was in the fields when I heard machine guns and I saw through the trees how people were falling down dead. I saw fire from the village huts, so I ran away to escape in the jungle.' (*The Times*, August 6). And there is the old man Peter Pringle met who lived with his three wives and nine children in a village about four or five kilometres from Wiriyamu. He remembered aircraft coming overhead and making strikes at Wiriyamu. His own village was not attacked but the inhabitants fled in fear. Pringle asked him to name those he knew had died in Wiriyamu and about a dozen names he and his wives mentioned checked against the published report (*Sunday Times*, August 5). And there is chief Trabuco of a neighbouring village to which the Chawola survivors first fled. He visited the burnt out ruins the next day, the 17th and counted the bodies. "After I counted them I ran away because I was frightened". (*Daily Telegraph*, August 20).

But there were also a few people who had actually been present and escaped wounded, and a group of these from Chawola quickly arrived at the mission of San Pedro. There was Antonio, a fifteen-year-old boy with his little brother of four years, Domingos; there was Antonio's friend Manuel; there was Tembo, a five-year-old; there was Serina, a thirteen-year-old girl; and there was a young married women Podista. All could report the deaths of most other members of their families: Antonio of his father and mother, a brother and sister; Serina, her father and mother and nine other members of the family; Podista, her husband and three year old son; Tembo, his father and mother and two brothers: Family after family nearly exterminated.

There had been massacres before but nothing which the Tete missionaries knew on this scale. Just as Fr Valverde had composed as precise reports as he was able of the atrocities in the Mucumbura district, so now the fathers in and around San Pedro resolved to write an exact account of what had taken place. The subsequent reports were most carefully compiled by the fathers as a group on the basis of eye witness evidence, but Fr José Sangalo took a chief hand in writing them; he was assisted by Vicente Berenguer and others.

A first report was completed only three days later, Tuesday, December 19. It concerned Chawola and was a very simple document based on the reports of the group of survivors already mentioned. It contained the names of forty-two victims. The production of an adequate report about what happened in and around Wiriyamu proved a lengthier business, because the atrocities there had a less simple character, the number of victims was much bigger, and a group of survivors from the village did not come straight to San Pedro. It took the Fathers three weeks to produce their second report which was completed on January 6 and included the names of 138 victims. It was based not only on the evidence of survivors, but also on that of members of the Portuguese forces themselves, both white and black, some of whom had been horrified by the bestiality of these events. But while they included the names of witnesses in the first document, the priests decided that this was to put people in peril and so left them out of the second.

The text of the two reports which follow is as they were sent to the London Office of Amnesty International on June 11. It is an exact translation of the Portuguese original of which twenty-six copies were made from a stencil at a Tete mission in January for dispatch to the bishops and other authorities.

I. The Chawola Report

The Massacre of Chief Gandali. Saturday, December 16, 1972
At about 2.00 pm, two jets bombarded the hamlets of Wiriyamu and Juwau, some twenty-five km from the city of Tete. These hamlets were part of the native kingdom of Chief Gandali.

At the same time, five helicopters landed armed troops, who surrounded the hamlets and machine-gunned the people, who were fleeing from the bombs. The hamlets were large, but we do not know how many people survived. What we do know is that the hamlets themselves were wiped out and raised to the ground.

The people of the hamlet of Chawola, very near to Wiriyamu and Juwau, seeing the flames from the bombs and the burning huts, gathered, terrified, in the quadrangle of their hamlet. Soon afterwards, they found themselves surrounded by troops, who rushed in, firing. The people tried to run away, but the soldiers gathered them up again. At once, the soldiers sacked the huts (stealing money, clothes, radios, and so on). Then they forced the people to clap their hands, so as to say goodbye to life, since they were about to die. The people obeyed. While they clapped their hands, the soldiers opened fire on them, shooting down men, women and children. They gathered up the bodies, covered them with straw, and set fire to them.

While the soldiers were setting fire to the huts, some of the people, who had only been wounded, managed to get away from the burning pyre. Some of them died in the bush, others are still hospitalized.

The day after these massacres, in the quadrangle of Chawola alone, fifty-three bodies were found. The following were identified:

1 Chawola
2 Mwataika (wife of Chawola)
3 Xavier (a youth, brother of Chawola)
4 Mixoni
5 Firipa (wife of Mixoni)
6 Luciano (adult son of Mixoni)
7 Rita (seven-year-old daughter of Mixoni)
8 Irisoni
9 Soza (wife of Irisoni)
10 Liria (wife of Irisoni)
11 Posi (one-month-old child of Irisoni, a girl)
12 Chinai (eight-year-old son of Irisoni)
13 Tsapwe nine-year-old son of Irisoni)
14 Luiza (nine-year-old daughter of Irisoni)
15 Chipiri (eight-year-old son of Irisoni)
16 Remadi (married son of Irisoni)
17 Luisa (wife of Remadi)
18 Manuel (one-year-old son of Remadi)
19 Akimo
20 Joana (wife of Akimo)
21 Birifi
22 M'balanyama (wife of Birifi)
23 Kapenu (seven-year-old son of Birifi)

24 Mataka (nine-year-old son of Birifi)
25 Batista
26 Asseria (wife of Batista)
27 Makau (eight-year-old son of Batista)
28 Sabudu (three-year-old son of Batista)
29 Mdeka
30 Firipa (wife of Mdeka)
31 Adamu (ten-year-old son of Mdeka)
32 Mchenga
33 Chifanikiso (three-year-old son of Mchenga)
34 Kunesa
35 Julio (fifteen-year-old son of Kunesa)
36 Marko
37 Pinto (aged eleven)
38 Mayeza (aged nine)
39 Mundani
40 Djipi (aged nine)
41 Nsembera
42 Pita.

(a)   All these facts were told to us by those survivors who were able to get out of the pyre and who are in hospital in Tete, and by others who managed to escape in time.

(b)   The identification of bodies was carried out by people who went to the ruined hamlets for that purpose.

(c)   Those who managed to get out of the pyre were

1 Antonio (fifteen-year-old son of Mixoni)
2 Domingos (four-year-old son of Mixoni)
3 Serina (thirteen-year-old daughter of Irisoni)
4 Tembo (five-year-old son of Batista)
5 Manuel (fifteen-year-old son of Mwantulujali)
6 Podista (wife of Mchenga).

If we made an enquiry supported by the authorities, we would be able to know if the number of the dead in all the demolished hamlets surpasses 300, as the people insist.

If there was no massacre, if a 'terrorist' base was destroyed, if children from one to ten years old are 'terrorists,' if old men and women, and women with children in their arms are 'terrorists,' then no one would be afraid to open a public enquiry to verify the truth of these massacres!

If all that happened was the destruction of a camp of 'turras'[1] and if a camp of 'turras' is not the same thing as a traditional hamlet, where men, women and children live; where they have their corn, their work and their clothes, and so on, then let us go to the spot where those hamlets stood, where they existed with all their inhabitants and their belongings, and let us meet the truth! Which is that it was not a 'terrorist' camp that was destroyed, but a group of hamlets and their defenceless population.

Tete, December 19, 1972

PS. At the time when we were completing this report, we learned that massacres were still going on in other hamlets, like those of Luis, Corneta and others, as far as Gama, in the kingdom of Chief Rego.

II. The Wiriyamu Report

We have been looking for signs of the truth.

Despite difficulties—some of them imposed on us, others circumstantial—in drawing up a full list of the names of the victims of the massacre of the populations of Wiriyamu and Juwau, the sources of the detailed information we have collected give us the right to maintain the affirmation that more than 400 victims fell— probably around 500.

Our research has enabled us to verify the following:—

During the afternoon of December 16, 1972, as we have said in the first part of our report, the hamlets of Wiriyamu and Juwau suffered a military raid by the forces of law and order.

After the bombardment, the commandos, brought there by helicopter who had surrounded the hamlets, ferociously invaded them increasing the terror of the inhabitants who were already panicking because of the bombs.

Once they were inside the hamlets, the commandos immediately began to sack the huts, and then massacred the people, in an excess of cruelty.

1 An army nickname for Frelimo.

A group of soldiers rounded up a number of the inhabitants in a courtyard, in order to shoot them. The people were forced to sit down, in two groups, men, on one side, and women on the other, so that each group had a good view of the other one being felled by bullets.

A soldier motioned whoever he wished (man, woman or child) to stand up, to come away from the group and as they did so, they were shot, one by one. This was the procedure that caused the greatest number of victims. Many children died in the arms of their mothers.

Thus, among many others, the soldiers killed:

1 Dzedzereke (adult male)
2 Mafita (his wife)
3 Kufuniwa (his adolescent son)
4 Birista (adult female)
5 Luwo (two-year-old boy)
6 Lekerani (adult male)
7 Sinoria (his wife)
8 Chamdindi (his five-year-old son)
9 Nguiniya (adult female)
10 Firipi (adult male)
11 Bziyeze (his wife)
12 Fete (his four-year-old son)
13 Meza (his one-year-old son)
14 Thangweradulo (his adolescent son)
15 Zerista (adult female)
16 Bwezani (adult male)
17 Aqueria (adult female)
18 Khapitoni (adult male)
19 Bunitu (his wife)
20 Mamaria (his wife)
21 Tinta (his adult son)
22 Chawene (his two-year-old son)
23 Chinai (his four-year-old son)
24 Kuoniwa (his twelve-year-old son)
25 Liyanola (adult female)
26 Djemuse (adult male)

27 Julia (adult female)
28 Djipi (nine-year-old boy)
29 Alista (adult female)
30 Mtsimpho (adult male)
31 Nsemberembe (nine-year-old boy)
32 Vira (adult female)
33 Thomasi (adult male)
34 Artencia (thirteen-year-old girl)
35 Duwalinya (adult female)
36 Sadista (adult female)
37 Florinda (adult female)
38 Siria (adult female)
39 Saizi (adult male)
40 Maviranti (his wife)
41 Domingos (his five-year-old son)
42 Maloza (his wife)
43 Sederia (his young daughter)
44 Mboi (his six-year-old daughter)
45 Gwaninifuwa (adult male)
46 Kachigamba (four-year-old boy)
47 Kuxupika (adult male)
48 Manyanyi (his wife)
49 Mapalata (his wife)
50 Cirio (his five-year-old son)
51 Kutonguiwa (adult man)
52 Maria (his three-year-old daughter)
53 Olinda (ten-year-old girl)
54 Lainya (adult female)
55 Luwina (adult female)
56 Aluviyana (adult female)
57 Kuitanti (adult male)
58 Caetano (five-year-old boy)
59 Kuchepa (twelve-year-old boy)
60 Bziuzeyani (adult female)
61 Djinja (adult male)
62 Alufinati (adult male)
63 Zabere (fourteen-year-old girl)

64   Aesta (sixteen-year-old girl)
65   Rosa (fifteen-year-old girl)
66   Zaberia (sixteen-year-old girl)
67   Alista (fourteen-year-old girl)
68   Mbiriyadende (adult male)
69   Guideria (adult female)
70   Khembo (adult male)
71   Kamuzi (two-year-old boy)
72   Chintheya (four-year-old girl)
73   Sunturu (adult male, brother of Kuxupika)
74   Dziwani (twelve-year-old boy)
75   Zeca (twelve-year-old boy)
76   Magreta (adult female)
77   Dinho (daughter of Magreta, aged two)
78   Hortencia (adult female, sister of Magreta)
79   Mario (ten-year-old brother of Magreta)
80   Chuva (adult male)
81   Kirina (wife of Chuva)
82   Fuguete (adult male)
83   Rita (four-year-old girl)
84   Eduardo (seven-year-old boy)
85   Tembo (three-year-old boy)

'Well Done!'

A woman called Vaina was told to stand up. She did so, with her little child Xanu in her arms—a nine-month-old baby. She fell, pierced by a bullet. The child disengaged itself and sat down next to its dead mother, crying frantically, but no one was able to help it. A soldier stepped forward, and it seemed he was going to comfort it. What a disillusion! Before the horrified eyes of the people, the soldier kicked the child brutally, slashing its head open. 'Shut up, dog!' he said. The prostrate child was no longer crying. It was dead. The soldier turned around, his boot covered with blood. His companions applauded him. 'Well done!' they shouted, 'You're a brave man!' That was the start of a macabre game of football, for his companions followed his example. And this way, several other children died, kicked to death by the soldiers.

The soldiers were accompanied by some DGS agents, who helped out with the killing. One of them called Chico Kachavi, who seemed to be the leader of the group, before finally killing his victims, started out by punching them with his fists until they fell down, exhausted. Then he would fire the 'coup de grace.'

Among others, the following died in this manner:

1 Kupensar (adult male)
2 Chaphuka (adult male)
3 Djoni (adult male)

Other soldiers, who wandered around the hamlets, forced people to go inside their huts, which they then set on fire, and people burned to death inside them.

Sometimes, before setting fire to the huts, they threw grenades inside, that exploded among the victims. Then they would set fire to the huts. In this fashion, among others, the following died:

1 Chakupendeka (old man)
2 Bwambuluka (his aged wife)
3 Kulinga (adult male, son of Cahekuendeka)
4 Naderia (Kulinga's wife)
5 Luwa (Kulinga's two-year-old daughter)
6 Marialena (Kulinga's two-year-old-daughter)
7 Tembo (Kulinga's eight-month-old son)
8 Keresiya (adult female)
9 Joaozinho (her two-year-old son)
10 Melota (her two-month-old son)
11 Kamchembere (one-month-old son)
12 Masalambani (six-year-old boy)
13 Chinai (five-year-old boy)
14 Domingos (five-year-old boy)
15 Mboy (ten-month-old girl)
16 Chiposi (three-year-old boy)
17 Augusto (one-year-old boy)
18 Farau (two-month-old boy)
19 Antonio (six-year-old boy)
20 Anguina (adult female)
21 Jantar (adult male)

22 Luisa (four-year-old girl)
23 Matias (two-year-old boy)
24 Nkhonde (one-year-old boy)
25 Xanu (seven-year-old boy)
26 Djoni (adult male)
27 Chawene (four-year-old boy)
28 Lodiya (adult female)
29 Mario (five-year-old boy)
30 Fostina (adult female)
31 Rosa (four-year-old girl)
32 Maria (two-year-old girl)
33 Boy (three-year-old boy)

'You'll Soon Know!'

The soldiers, while they ransacked the hamlet, found a woman, named Zostina, who was pregnant. They asked her what the sex was of the child she was carrying. 'I don't know,' she answered. 'You'll soon know,' they said. And, at once, with their knives they ripped her belly open, yanking out her intestines and her womb and showing her the foetus, which was struggling convulsively, and said 'There! Now do you know?' Then, mother and child were consumed by the flames.

Other soldiers amused themselves by killing children, grabbing them by the legs and bashing them against the ground or trees. Among several other children, the following died in this way:

1 Domingos (one-month-old boy)
2 Xanu (two-year-old boy)
3 Kulewa (three-year-old boy)
4 Chipiri (two-year-old boy)
5 Chuma (four-year-old girl)
6 Makonda (two-year-old boy)
7 Marko (one-year-old boy)
8 Luisa (four-year-old boy)
9 Mario (four-year-old boy)
10 Raul (four-year-old boy)

Many people were led to their death outside the hamlets. The following day, many bodies of young adolescents and

children from eleven to fifteen years old were found at the river
Nyamtawatawa. The bodies were mutilated and unrecognizable,
and it was not possible to identify them. Many of them had slit
throats, others fractured skulls. The bodies were in different positions: some heaped up; others lying down, next to one another;
others sitting, but buried up to their waists; most of them, however,
were spread out along the riverside.

There were signs that a macabre game had taken place before
the victims had been massacred. Was a Roman amphitheatre
game re-invented? There are no survivors to explain it.

'No one else will enjoy you.'

A fairly large group of soldiers dragged four maidens to a hiding
place where they were cruelly massacred after having been brutally
raped. 'No one else will enjoy you,' said the soldiers in triumphant
tones, full of hatred. They ripped off their 'misangas,' (a female
undergarment worn around the waist). The soldiers carried the
misangas as trophies around their necks.

The maidens slaughtered this way were:

1 Duzeria
2 Cecilia
3 Faliosa
4 Domina

'Suck it!'

Chintheya, a four-year-old girl, was crying, terrified. A soldier,
pretending to be sorry for her, went up to her and, fondling the
child, asked her if she was hungry. Without waiting for a reply,
he went on: 'Here's your bottle . . .' And he shoved the barrel
of his rifle into the child's mouth, saying 'Suck it!' And he fired.
The child fell with a gaping hole in the back of her head.

Chintheya was not the only victim to whom this treatment was
meted out; several others suffered the same fate.

'Phani Wense!' (Kill them all!)

A voice with authority had shouted repeatedly: 'Phani wense!'—
'Kill them all!' 'Leave no survivors.' It was the voice of the

DGS agent, Chico Kachavi.

A witness says that an army officer suggested that they be merciful, and take those poor people to an 'aldeamento'. But the sinister voice of Agent Chico was heard, louder and more furiously: 'These are the orders from our chief'—he said 'Kill them all. The ones spared are the ones who denounce us.'

Two children from those hamlets, found casually after the massacre had been carried out, were burned in cold blood inside a hut by that same DGS agent, on the pretext that they might denounce the troops.

That afternoon, in Wiriyamu and Juwau, all one could hear were the yells of the soldiers, the rifle shots, the moans of the victims dying of their wounds. The people of Wiriyamu and Juwau lived through moments of the most appalling anguish.

These scenes went on until sunset. By then, the soldiers were tired of such brutality. So, then, some victims managed to escape death, by fleeing. It is they who, as eye witnesses, have given us many of the details we have described here, and which, therefore, we state to be authentic.

Furthermore, the Tete Health Committee, which went to the place of the massacre about twenty days later (much too late, therefore) to verify matters, has not denied our report.

Today, the charred remains of the hamlets of Wiriyamu, Juwau and Chawola and the human skeletons which lie on their soil are incontrovertible evidence of the bloody drama that plunged the people of Mchenga and Nyamphangala into mourning.

We need hardly say that the inhuman actions committed by those soldiers are genocidal acts, which deserve the reprobation of all men of sane mind.

Tete, January 6, 1973

*   *   *

The Bishop of Tete, Dom Augusto Cesar Ferriera da Silva, had been away from Tete on December 16. As soon as he returned he was presented by his priests with an account of what had happened and urged to press for a full inquiry. He certainly went to the Governor, Colonel Videira, and it was probably due to him that Doctor José da Paz of the hospital in Tete was permitted to send representatives of a Tete health committee to fly over Wiriyamu in a helicopter some twenty days later and observe the unburied bodies. They included a Spanish nun, Sister Lucia, and an African nurse named Fonseca. The bishop had no doubt as to what had happened. It was in fact he who first informed Fr Julio Moure of the news—at supper in Beira—and he told a lawyer in Lourenco Marques in January that he had been forced to complain about the lack of burial for over 300 bodies around Wiriyamu. The written reports were of course presented by the missionaries to the bishop as to the whole Episcopal Conference of Mozambique. Massacres had indeed taken place before but a massacre of this size only just outside a large town and fifteen miles away from a bishop's residence with a full report on it, whose substantial accuracy the bishop was apparently ready to vouch for, was another matter, and the board of bishops felt in duty bound to register a common protest. They did so on March 31 in a letter to the Governor General of Mozambique: 'Having heard details, which are being circulated, of the events which took place within the Chief Gandali regions, not far from the city of Tete, during the month of December last—events according to which hundreds of people, some of them absolutely innocent, might have lost their lives through the action of the armed forces . . . We cannot but express our most vehement indignation and protest.'

This letter, however, was not published—few people knew of its existence. It and the brief non-committal reply from the Governor-General remained in fact pieces of paper and no more. The Governor-General claimed that an inquiry was being conducted into the charges but no one on the spot ever heard of the inquiry or was asked to give evidence.

Copies of the two reports, sometimes together, sometimes separate, individually typed and retyped with the little variations that so easily slip in during such a process, were circulated in church circles in the country. As the weeks passed, it was clear that there was to be no official investigation on the part of the government, no public protest on the part of the Church. But what was to be done? Even to get a copy out of the country was difficult. In fact two Burgos fathers, Julio Moure and Miguel Buendia, were expelled from Mozambique on February 20. They had been working in Beira diocese, not Tete, and so had themselves no close knowledge of the massacres. A copy of the Wiriyamu report (but not that of Chawola) was slipped into Fr Buendia's hands an hour before leaving by plane. Despite a ninety-minute search the police failed to find it. It alone was taken to Madrid, to the Superior General of the Burgos Fathers. Priests of other societies, however, were also working in Tete; and a full copy of both reports had reached Fr Bertulli, in Rome by the beginning of May—the Vatican Secretariat of State had probably received a copy through the nuncio still earlier but of that we cannot be sure. Fr Bertulli rightly felt that the first thing to do was to bring this to the attention of Portuguese authority in Lisbon and see what action it was prepared to take. He therefore confronted Senhor Bonifacio de Miranda, a minister in the Lisbon government, with the report at a public meeting at Kamen in Germany, May 12 and 13. Sr Miranda simply shrugged the massacre off as the work of Frelimo—hardly a plausible explanation for a major operation just outside a large town. German journalists present ignored the whole story.

Fr Bertulli next attempted to publish the story in Italy and the full text of both the Chawola and Wiriyamu reports was published by the Cablo Press in Rome on June 4. The world's alert newsmen continued to take no notice whatsoever. A week later, June 11, still quite unknown to me, a full copy of both the reports sent by Fr Bertulli was received by Amnesty International in London.

That was how things stood when I visited Spain for four days, June 18-22. I went for quite another reason: I had been invited to read a paper on reciprocal inter-communion to the Anglican—Roman Catholic Joint West European Working Group which was meeting in Salamanca. The paper has since been published in the Autumn number of the quarterly *One in Christ*. It was my first visit to Spain, but I had met members of the Burgos missionary society elsewhere, notably in Rhodesia where a large group of them work and where I had been lecturing in a number of dioceses in April and May 1973. I had heard that their priests had great difficulties in Mozambique and that two of them had been in prison in Lourenco Marques for over a year. I wanted to know more, because the prime minister of Portugal, Marcello Caetano, was due in London within a month to celebrate the sixth centenary of the Anglo-Portuguese alliance and I had been asked by the Catholic Institute for International Relations to make a speech at a luncheon given on the occasion of the centenary celebrations in which I would analyze the Portuguese position in Africa and its connections with the Catholic Church.

I had lunch with the Superior General of the society, Fr Artazcoz, and again, on returning from Salamanca, with Fr Anoveros, another senior man and the editor of their missionary review, to which I had already contributed more than one article. In the course of our discussions I was fascinated to learn that they possessed a number of very detailed documents about the current situation in Mozambique and in particular massacres at Mucumbura and Wiriyamu. I asked for copies. They had no spare ones available, but promised to send me some as soon as possible. Fr Anoveros put them into the post on June 27 and I received them about three days later. They included the full text of the report of Valverde and Hernandez on the 1971 Mucumbura massacres, and the Wiriyamu report. But they did not include the Chawola report which had never been received in Madrid and about which Fr Anoveros knew nothing—and so neither did I. In Madrid I had also met Julio Moure, but I had not seen Vicente Berenguer who had returned to Spain in April and was of course, one of the report's authors. But he was not in Madrid at the time.

When I received the Wiriyamu report at the very end of June together with much other material, I quite quickly realized its importance. Accounts of the Mucumbura massacres had in fact, as I knew, already appeared in the *Observer* and elsewhere, and had made little impression. But they had after all happened back in 1971, while this had taken place only just over six months before, and it was not a matter of a dozen or two people but hundreds. I had made no concrete plan with the Burgos fathers —they gave me the documents because I was interested, with permission to publish them, a job difficult enough in Spain. I had no plan until I had seen them: probably they would just constitute matter for an article in a church paper and some extra information for my CIIR speech.

Studying the Wiriyamu report convinced me that here was something different. I had the greatest confidence in the reliability of the Burgos fathers. They seemed to me, both those I had seen at work in Rhodesia and those I had met in Madrid, a fine and extremely disinterested group of men. They clearly take a mastery of African languages very seriously indeed. They are men who have committed themselves for life to the service of God and their fellow men, and have done so with obvious vigour, cheerfulness and simplicity of life. One or another might be unreliable but that a whole group of them, countenanced by their Superior General, should put out a false report of this kind seemed to me quite inconceivable. And the report itself, in its simplicity, its straight forward statement of fact, its precision in naming place, date and individuals, bore the hall-mark of truth. If much of the detail was horrifying, that was unfortunately no reason whatsoever for thinking it not true. Such things have happened in more than one country of late. But if it was true, and still more if being true the Portuguese Government had done nothing whatsoever to investigate its charges or punish the culprits, then its significance was immense. It had got to be published. I cabled Madrid for confirmation of the permission to publish and at the same time gave it to a translator. That was on July 5. I received a reply the next day, Friday the 6th and rang up Louis Heren of the *Times* that evening. I felt the *Times* was the most suitable place to publish it, but I wanted it printed in full, not made into a general article based upon it. Heren told me to send it to him and I did so the next day. The *Times* received it on Monday the 9th and published it with an editorial on the 10th. They too were rightly convinced of its reliability and its major importance.

In a way it was accidental that the report was published a week before Caetano arrived in London. It was published when it was because that was when I received it and at once resolved that it must be published. There never was less of a plot. I had no connexion with the 'End the Alliance' campaign, none with Frelimo, none with the Labour Party. The Burgos Fathers themselves were naturally not very conscious of the importance of Caetano's visit to England—few of them can even speak English. Even the Catholic Institute for International Relations was not too enthusiastic about it: its staff felt that I would be diverting their long-prepared lunch, intended to consider the wider issues of the Anglo-Portuguese alliance, into something far too narrow. 'One more massacre', said its general secretary, 'Who will be interested in that anyway?' I did not agree, but it was a personal decision. Hard facts can in my view be more illuminating than oceans of theory, and here I felt were some very hard facts. One hundred and thirty names might move mountains. The *Times* agreed. But of course if Caetano had not been coming the next week, the press and public opinion might hardly have reacted at all, anymore than it did to Bertulli's efforts. We must be very grateful to Caetano for enabling us so providentially to manifest to the whole world the extreme wickedness of present Portuguese government in Mozambique. In my bones I knew it was dynamite, and the weekend of the 8th I felt like Guy Fawkes sitting by his gunpowder barrels, but I certainly didn't foresee how vast the explosion was to be.

It was only on the afternoon of Monday, July 9 that I knew the report of the Wiriyamu massacre would be in the *Times* of the next day—unless the threatened printers strike intervened. I had driven down to attend a small conference at Ammerdown Park, a fairly remote corner of Somerset. On the 11 o'clock news that night I heard for sure there would be papers on the morrow. By 8 am the BBC was on the phone. The storm had begun and for the next ten days it did not stop. I was carried along in a whirlwind of activity. This was really quite unexpected. I had not foreseen how vast the reaction would be and how largely everything would depend upon me—my credibility, clarity and the firmness with which I held to my position. By lunchtime I had given a TV interview and three Radio interviews in Bristol. When I arrived back in Birmingham at teatime I found the College of the Ascension where I lived had been besieged all day by the press. I gave a hurried interview and took the train to London. The hour and a half between Birmingham and Euston was a useful time for evaluating the crisis which I now fully realized had broken around me. I had to be quite clear about my position and then step neither forwards nor backwards. Harold Wilson had called for the cancellation of Caetano's visit. The 'End the Alliance' Campaign would redouble its efforts; if Caetano came there would be a multitude of demonstrations. The Portuguese Embassy, on its side, had flatly denied the story: the very place Wiriyamu did not exist—it could not be found on the map.

When I reached Euston a barrage of cameras and reporters was awaiting me. Despite the excitement, the novelty and the importance of it all, I found it also rather funny. Anyway the TV people carried me away, first for an interview for the ITA News and then for two interviews with the BBC. The next day was to be the CIIR luncheon at Chatham Home—the occasion which had in a sense caused it all. It had been excellently prepared. Mario Soares, the chief Portuguese opposition leader living in exile in Paris, and Lord Caradon, were to be the chief speakers, and I was the third man—chosen to represent the viewpoint of the Catholic Institute itself. We had a supper planned that Tuesday night to finalize arrangements at the flat of Mildred Nevile, the Secretary General. I only got there long after 10 pm, and there was still a cameraman, and a representative of Belgian Radio waiting to see me. It was an excited little gathering with all the CIIR people, Mario Soares, Antonio De Figueiredo and their wives, Tom Burns of the *Tablet* and Hugh O'Shaughnessy and Margaret Feeny of the Africa Centre. It was now clear the luncheon would have a rather different character from that which had been originally intended.

The next day, the 11th, Wiriyamu was the top front page news in every national paper from the headlines of the *Times*: 'Mr Heath will not call off Portuguese State visit: Massacre denied by Lisbon' through the *Guardian's* 'Atrocity storm turns heat on

Caetano visit,' the *Daily Mail's* 'Storm over "Massacre" and the *Daily Express's* ' "Massacre" Uproar.' to the *Sun's* 'Don't let this Dictator into Britain!' Fury over visit by "Massacre" Premier', and the *Daily Mirror's* 'This Man is not Welcome.'

The *Evening Standard* was on the phone as I scrambled out of bed in the Sheehys' house in Baalbec Street. It was to be another extraordinary day. At our luncheon in Chatham House and in the press conference immediately afterwards I realized for the first time how bitter the opposition was going to be. The Portuguese lobby and the *Telegraph* seemed determined to undermine both me and the report. Patrick Wall said the meeting was unworthy of the CIIR because all three speakers were critical of Portugal. Did I claim to speak in the name of the Catholic Church, he wanted to know. Why, demanded Lady Listowel, did we not protest about the atrocities in Burundi? Bishop Colin Winter asked me to withdraw a statement which I had made to the effect that, notwithstanding Wiriyamu, the Portuguese rule was still in some ways better than that of South Africa. The atmosphere was extremely tense and I spoke both fast and furious— coldly furious. I agreed with Bishop Winter that in some ways the Portuguese rule was indeed worse than South Africa's—I did not think such a massacre likely to happen in South Africa. Perhaps I was wrong. The point is that the two kinds of tyranny though linked are still somewhat different. The Prime Minister of Burundi is not making a state visit to Britain, I pointed out to Judith Listowel; nor have we an ancient alliance with Burundi; nor has the Catholic Church a Concordat with the Government of Burundi. No, I said to Mr Wall, I speak only for myself and have never suggested anything else. What I wanted to do in that speech was to stress the special English Catholic responsibility in regard to Portugal's tyranny—English because of the traditional alliance, Catholic because of the Concordat and the very privileged position the Catholic Church occupies as a result in Portuguese Africa. I did not appeal for an end to the alliance—the alliance is between two peoples, and the Portuguese people today are mostly as oppressed as any. What we objected to — I was speaking here for the CIIR who had organized the luncheon—was friendship with their fascist government.

Immediately after the meeting a lady introduced herself: Mrs Isobel Turner, a Portuguese lawyer and journalist now living in England. She said she had heard of a major massacre near Tete already in January from a Portuguese friend (I have his name) who had been in Tete in late December. It was a valuable piece of confirmatory evidence from a wholly independent source.

The press conference was even more of a strain: I faced a host of journalists and a battery of cameras. Sharp hostility and disbelief in some quarters were quite unveiled. How could I be so sure? Either I must admit to uncertainty or to having a 'closed mind.' I would agree to neither, but it clearly was a difficulty that I could not say exactly where Wiriyamu was—in the province of Tete, yes; in the area of San Pedro mission, yes. But where exactly was that? This was the worst chink in my armour, and in a hasty little conference with Mildred Nevile, Tim Sheehy and Hugh O'Shaughnessy immediately afterwards we decided that I must go back to Madrid at once to settle that point. The *Sunday Times* had offered to send me there to acquire additional information and we decided that I should leave the next morning. There were still four more television interviews to follow that day—with BBC and German TV at Chatham House and then, much later in the evening, Italian and Dutch TV teams turned up at my sister's house in Twickenham. It had been a long day.

The next morning the newspapers were as full as ever of the affair and the letters on it were now filling up the *Times* correspondence columns. Brigadier Michael Calvert, well-known for his reports on how Portugal is winning the war, declared that 'there is a secret section of the Jesuit fraternity who have thrown in their lot with proponents of world terrorism.' I wonder how he knows? As neither I nor the Burgos Fathers have anything to do with the Jesuits, it wasn't very obviously relevant anyway. 'I consider' he went on, 'that Fr Adrian Hastings' allegations (so aptly timed and politically and obviously not religiously motivated) can be placed on a par with some of the wilder allegations of certain bemused Irish priests in Ulster who are so emotionally disorientated that they think that the end justifies the means.' Portugal's methods of dealing with the revolt, Brigadier Calvert claimed, 'far surpass in sympathy, humanity and compassion for their enemies any other counter-insurgency policies.' Others claimed, on the contrary, that the report of the massacre should have caused no surprise—Portugal's ruthless treatment of dissidents was already only too well-known. This was the view of several Portuguese correspondents. So Mr. José da Fonseca wrote, 'As an ordinary Portuguese citizen and army deserter, I would like to thank you for publishing Fr A. Hastings' report on the Wiriyamu massacre.' And so it went on.

That morning I flew to Madrid. Fr Artazcoz, Superior General of the Burgos Fathers, met me at the airport with Fr Miguel Antoni, an oldish man who had worked in the San Pedro mission for years and was Mozambique regional superior of the society until he left in March 1973. He had been to Wiriyamu many times, he said, and would willingly identify it to any International Commission. He explained at once exactly where it was. A quiet person, not expelled from Mozambique, he had no desire to get into the limelight and tended to slip away when journalists were around. When we reached the house in Garcia Morato, there was a good deal of excitement and a BBC man on the spot when we arrived was just about to carry off a small film Fr Font had taken in Mozambique. I felt that order must be established at once and plans discussed before anything further was done, so to his chagrin the BBC man had to relinquish the film and was told to come back at 3 o'clock.

The film question was quickly settled. Fr Artazcoz and I looked at it. Once Fr Font explained that it had been taken in the north western area of Tete in August 1969, we realized it was quite useless to let it be shown, and could be dangerous. When our friend returned I explained this; he was very annoyed and to console him I said I would take the film back to England myself and if the BBC still wanted to use it, they could approach me but I would have to explain first what it actually showed.

Denis Herbstein of the *Sunday Times* joined us and together we went over a great deal of information. Next morning I returned to England, to be met at Heathrow by various journalists and a young man sent from the BBC to collect the film. I was surprised about this. I told the journalists I had no statement to make but was thoroughly satisfied with my visit to Madrid and fully confident of the truth of the report. They heard me speaking of the film with the BBC fellow and presumed this was new evidence I had brought back. I allowed him to take the film to have a look at it but explained its date and gave them no permission to use it. There was no car waiting for me and we went together in the BBC one, first to my sister's house in Twickenham and then on into the town. They dropped me at the *Sunday Times* office for which I was grateful.

It was a pleasure working with John Barry and Peter Pringle of the *Insight* team that Friday evening and much of Saturday. They wrote the text—an excellent survey of the whole background to the Wiriyamu report—while I made suggestions and corrected occasional inaccuracies.

The BBC had meanwhile sent me back the film predictably saying it was of no use. Fair enough. At 1.30 am on Saturday morning I was woken by the telephone. It was the *Times* to ask the truth about the film. The *Telegraph* had published an account suggesting that I had brought it back as decisive new evidence of the massacre and the BBC had rejected it, having 'discovered' that it was four years old. I was very angry. As this story went on being repeated I had publicly to request the BBC to state that it was I who told them the date of the film and that I had given them no permission to use it, and of course they did so (*The Times,* July 17).

On returning from Madrid I had said that my findings would be published in the *Sunday Times*. In a way they were in the *Insight* article; but I had also my personal reply to make, in the light of the greater information I now possessed, to the many critics of the last week. Much of the material of the attack had been repeated in the *Sunday Telegraph,* so I spent the middle of that Sunday composing a long letter which the *Times* published the next morning. Mildred Nevile drove me to their offices and, while there, I was able to meet Louis Heren for the first time.

All through the long affair I was immensely helped by the loyal support of the *Times* staff. They too, of course, had been under attack for publishing an 'unsubstantiated rumour.' If one is going to be suddenly plunged into a battle of this kind, it is certainly helpful to have the *Times* on one's side. That Monday, July 16, Marcello Caetano arrived in England. There is no point in describing the visit here. It is better to turn aside to analyze the counter-argument. Wiriyamu does not exist. It is unthinkable that 400 people should have been murdered last December and no news of it published before. Portuguese policy is to win the hearts of the people and they are doing so very successfully: so how could they spoil their good work by such an atrocity? Anyway, there is no 'evidence': Not one person who has been properly massacred has reported the fact afterwards so how can we know that he has? These reports are all 'second-hand'.

Portugal refused any international inquiry. It refused a public inquiry. It declared that it was making, had made, would make an inquiry into the allegations. But it did say that journalists could go and see for themselves. One man was off the mark remarkably quickly. It was Bruce Loudon for the *Telegraph* who lives in Lisbon. Day by day readers of the Telegraph were regaled with his intrepid exploits all over Mozambique. He must have left Lisbon within twenty-four hours of the *Times'* publication because his first report from a spot far away north of Mucumbura is in the *Telegraph* of the 13th. If he had inquired from the priests in Madrid first where Wiriyamu was, he would not perhaps have followed quite such an absurd goose chase, for it was in fact a well-known village only to near the town of Tete. He tells us firmly in his first report that 'there is no Mozambique place beginning with the letter "W".' His journalistic method was to arrive in an army helicopter and, having gathered together a native or two, then to ask them—across an army interpreter of course—whether the army had been committing any massacres round here recently. 'Did the army massacre your sisters, cousins and aunts last December?' No; 'Well thank you very much'. The conversation would seem to have gone much like that.

Loudon's prize piece, however, is to be found in the *Sunday*

Telegraph of July 15. Despite his remarks about 'W's' of two days before he now happily heads his article 'in Wiliamo south of Tete'. He declares that while 'there never has been a hamlet in the area of that name' (Wiriyamu), there is one called 'Wiliamo' —quite oblivious of the fact that the people in such a village did not spell the name anyway and that 'L' and 'R' are next to interchangeable in Bantu speech. Anyway he visited 'Wiliamo' which in the *Sunday Telegraph* he describes as ten kilometres southwest of Tete' (which Wiriyamu certainly is not), while in the *Daily Telegraph* of the next day he described it as 'seven miles south-east of Tete', which was a little nearer the truth. He described a burnt-out village whose inhabitants he claimed were 're-settled' in April in *aldeamentos*. He said he saw no sign of a massacre though he did admit that 'curiously the villagers frequently leave possessions such as cooking pots . . . what some members of our party did find a little strange, however, was that such items as bicycles and a bed and mattress had been left behind.' As such things are indeed quite the most valuable possessions the villagers can have had, it is indeed curious that when they were 'voluntarily' resettled they left them behind.

Was the village which Loudon and other journalists, including MacManus of the Guardian, were taken to 'with a heavy Portuguese Army escort' really Wiriyamu? possibly yes, but most probably no. By July the area was full of burnt out ruins with no inhabitants left and therefore unidentifiable except from the memory of a reliable person who knew the place previously. In the judgment of those who knew Wiriyamu previously it seems likely that they were taken to another hamlet in the area, rather less far away from Tete than Wiriyamu. No journalist spent more than a few hours in the country outside the town of Tete or was able really to reconnoitre the area.

When one recalls the repeated Portuguese denial in July that there ever was such a place as Wiriyamu, it was certainly instructive to hear, for instance, on September 14, Herr Todenhoffer, a Christian Democrat member of the German parliament, speak of his recent visit to Mozambique as a guest of the Portuguese government: 'Ich habe einmal Wiriyamu besichtigt—I visited

Wiriyamu.' This is only one instance in many of the complete rubbish, the self-contradictions, the blatant lies, that Portuguese government spokesmen have thought fit to publish.

Although journalists were to be allowed free access to Tete, in fact both Michael Knipe of the *Times* and Peter Pringle of the *Sunday Times* were expelled by the DGS after only three days there. But basically the conditions for a free journalistic inquiry were simply not present. No African in his senses would quickly speak out to a passing journalist about army atrocities when he and the army will remain, but the journalist, his story written, will fly away.

Great play was made with the Bishop of Tete's refusal to confirm the report of the massacre after the Burgos Fathers had claimed that he knew of it. The bishop's position was certainly a delicate one. The original report had been presented to him first of all; he had discussed it with his priests and later with the whole episcopal conference of Mozambique, which learnt that he had already taken up the matter both with the district authorities and with the governor general. The episcopal conference decided to write again to the latter: 'Because of the nature of such events, reprehensible at all levels and being more and more widespread with harmful repercussions in our midst, we joined our voices to that of the Bishop of Tete.' That was March 31. The to him unexpected publication of the matter in July and immediate uncompromising denial by the Portuguese government, put him in an extremely difficult position: to affirm it publicly was to make a direct personal challenge to the government with immense political and personal implications. Everyone realized the significance of the bishop's evidence. He had had no personal experience of the workings of a free press and felt, what was largely true, that the journalists who came to see him were simply trying to make politics either for or against the Portuguese government. He did not want to be used in this way—his whole background of a state Church was against it—and therefore refused either to confirm or deny the report. The implications of this position for the truth of the report were from the first clear enough: if it were untrue, if his own priests were falsely accusing the local government of such heinous crimes, he had the obvious obligation to say so, and no reason for not doing so. If, however, it was true, he could well feel that the prudential reasons for not committing himself to a public denial of what the government had said were more than adequate. His own proper episcopal protest, he could feel, had already been made in private and there was no need to repeat it to foreign journalists. Those whom the truth should concern already knew it. His own prior knowledge of the massacre has, of course, subsequently been made known to the world by the publication in September of the bishops' protest of March.

It would be useless to go over all the heated arguments of those days. It is quite impossible without a free and public inquiry to establish independently to the report, every detail that the report contains. But the substantial truth of a major massacre committed by the Portuguese troops south of Tete on December 16 was confirmed, first by the on-the-spot inquiry of Peter Pringle of the *Sunday Times* published in that paper on August 5. He was able to see a document dated 1968 which already named Wiriyamu. He was able to meet Antonio, one of the survivors of Chawola, and other people who had been nearby at the time. He would have learnt much more, if the political police had not confiscated his notes after three days and expelled him from Tete. He was getting far too near to the truth.

It was confirmed, secondly, by the publication of the full protest of the bishops in September. It is quite clear from that statement, despite its rather obsequious character, that the bishops were convinced in their own minds in March that a major atrocity had taken place. A third major confirmation came from the *Star* of Johannesburg on September 25, asserting that it had discovered from Portuguese sources through 'a great exercise in dogged investigative reporting' that up to a hundred people had been massacred on December 16 at Wiriyamu. Finally Frelimo has made its own investigation, names its own witnesses—Fernando Bero and Fernando Antonio Joao—and outlines the same basic story (*Observer*, October 7; *Times*, October 8).

We will see what light these various sources throw upon the accuracy of the original report a little later. Let us first return for a moment to my own experience.

I had no intention of joining in the demonstrations against Caetano's visit. Different people have different tasks. I would have been very disappointed if there had been no such demonstrations but my own work was a different one: it was to assert and reassert the truth of Wiriyamu, explaining it ever more fully in its context and implications. It was for others to decide what should be done in the light of that truth.

I was impressed by many of the journalists and newsmen with whom I came into contact. Even if they had known little about Mozambique previously several of them made quite an effort to find out now. The Sunday Times *Insight* men were particularly serious-minded in their approach: I had indeed already admired their work on Northern Ireland and elsewhere and it was a privilege to come into personal contact with them. And nearly all the journalists were polite and personally friendly. Some, however, appeared shoddy in their work; thus it was only too clear on occasions that men working professionally on this story had never carefully read even the original report, and claimed, for instance, that it named eighty-six victims when in fact it named a hundred and thirty. There were those who seemed committed to its refutation ing. Men from the *Telegraph* spent hours trying to establish that it was all part of 'a carefully orchestrated campaign,' a 'political plant.' They had to admit, in fact, that they found no evidence of such a thing, and there was none. But various journalists attempted to poke into my private life, wanted to know how much the *Sunday Times* had paid me and so forth. A man from the *Daily Express* rang me several times on July 16 to ask if I would accompany an *Express* expedition to Mozambique. As the *Express* had taken up a hostile position, I expressed surprise and doubted anyway whether the Portuguese could possibly admit me, but I affirmed my willingness to go on certain conditions, chief of which was that Fr Antoni from Madrid could come too. He promised to ring again within a few hours, but I never heard another word. Of course if I had refused to go, they could have published that fact to the world to undermine my credibility.

I realized more and more how dangerous the telephone is: a

newspaper rings one up at any odd moment, fires some (perhaps) unexpected questions and everything one says is recorded. But one has no recording apparatus on one's own side. When one is also very tired, battered by numerous pressures and without a secretary and previous experience of such a situation, it can become very tricky indeed. I was fortunate not to be tripped up. I owe a lot to the help I did get in those very difficult days from my family at Twickenham, the staff of the CIIR and colleagues at the College of the Ascension.

I was somewhat disappointed with the television authorities. I had several entirely fair interviews for the news on both BBC and ITA, but what one can say in those circumstances in answer to three or four straight questions—often the same question—is limited. It seemed to me that the matter was so important in itself and was receiving so extensive and continued coverage in the press that there should have been a longer TV programme of discussion at which I could put the position in full. But I was never asked in this country to take part in any such programme, although I did have long interviews for programmes of such a kind on the networks of several other countries. This is, I think, characteristic of the failure of BBC and ITA to give adequate serious coverage outside the news to major issues of current affairs.

My mail in those weeks became pretty extensive. One letter signed by 'Disgusted Roman Catholic' would attack me for complaining of massacres in Africa when the British army was doing the same and worse in Ulster. The next would denounce me as an IRA priest; the third, signed by Brezhnev, thanked me warmly for doing his work but reproved me for slipping up over the name 'Wiriyamu.' Others were full of pornographic and sadistic rubbish, generally pretty poorly spelt; many were unsigned, though a number of retired army officers felt they had to put in a word. Someone said what a good thing the massacre was, there would now be fewer black people to come to this country, and someone else sent a leaflet whose printed cover bore the words 'IT NEVER HAPPENED AFTER ALL!.' Oh, I thought, they have got into print pretty quick; but I was mistaken in that because the paper in question concerned 'the alleged Nazi massacre of six million Jews'. Some people attacked the pope and the Catholic Church, of which they felt I was a typical representative, and others attacked me for letting down the Catholic Church and the priesthood—getting involved in politics. One person felt it necessary to write and say that having seen my behaviour he now knew he was right to stop going to church fifteen years ago. A good many letters were on the lines of 'I would believe you if you had also protested against . . . . The invasion of Czechoslovakia, Bloody Sunday, the Katyn massacre, what have you. The prize in this line should be given to the gentleman who wrote to say he would believe me if I could show that I had protested when Mussolini invaded Ethiopia! Of course, if I had publicly protested about all these things, they would have replied that I was obviously a professional protester and therefore not to be relied upon. Many letters particularly, I am afraid, from Catholics, had a bitter, rather pathetic anti-Communist character: 'Yes, Fr Hastings, you should not wear that clerical frock, the one of a Russian Political commissioner fits you better.' ·

It was a relief and a real comfort to receive some letters of support as well—far fewer at first but they kept on coming while the hostile ones faded away more quickly. Many, of course, were from friends; others from people I had never met. Many of them were very kind, and it really was a help to get them at a time of very great stress. I was sad that not one single Catholic bishop felt able to write a word of personal encouragement, but an Anglican bishop did so and many priests of several churches.

For me one of the most consoling sides of the whole affair was the warm friendliness and gentle gratitude of a number of Portuguese people in this country and the United States, the first being Mario Soares. As one of them said to me: 'you can be sure that you are a better friend of the Portuguese people than the whole British Government put together.' I won't forget that.

David Steel of the Liberal Party asked me to speak on the subject to the Liberal MPs, and I did so in the House of Commons on July 18. Being a life-long Liberal I was delighted to have a chance to meet them but was not too impressed by their knowledge of

African affairs. As many of them have probably been in the Liberal Party for a dozen years or less, I think they were surprised when I said at the end that I was particularly glad to talk with them as my family had been unbrokenly Liberal since the late eighteenth century! The next day I flew to New York, to the UNO. It was the first time I had crossed the Atlantic and this rapid visit of thirty-six hours, entirely arranged by the United Nations, was almost a fantasy experience. Supping with Salim Salim, the Tanzanian ambassador, and Marcelino Dos Santos, the Vice-president of Frelimo; talking with numerous UN officials and, of course, a new bevy of journalists; above all being carried up to the 38th floor of the building for a personal interview with Secretary-General Waldheim — what wholly unexpected things had happened to me in these ten days!

It was a real pleasure to meet Waldheim. We had a quiet twenty-minute discussion in which he put a number of questions and listened very carefully to my replies. Afterwards he issued the following statement:

'It was with deep pain that I received the personal report of Father Hastings. His information based on the testimony of missionaries in Mozambique, has aroused the conscience of mankind.

'Over the past ten years numerous resolutions have been adopted by the General Assembly, the Security Council and the Special Committee of 24 calling on the Government of Portugal to cease "all acts of repression" against the people of Mozambique. The Security Council and the General Assembly have called upon that Government to enter into negotiations for the purpose of arriving at a peaceful solution based on the inalienable right of the people of Mozambique to freedom in accordance with the Charter of the United Nations and the resolutions of the General Assembly. I earnestly appeal to the Government of Portugal to follow this course.

'The Committee of 24 is today holding a special meeting to receive Father Hastings' testimony. I urge all Member States to lend their support to the committee in its inquiry into the tragic report that Faher Hastings has presented."

My interview with Waldheim was followed by a special meeting of the committee of 24 on decolonization. It began with a forty-minute statement by me on the massacre, its background, the evidence for it, and its significance. The whole thing was under the television cameras. I was followed by Dos Santos, whom I was meeting in New York for the first time. He outlined the wider situation in Mozambique and then thanked me warmly and personally for what I had done: 'Fr Hastings, kindly accept our feelings of friendship and appreciation and please allow us to tell you that your courage and honour are indeed a pride for your people.' Dos Santos was speaking in the name of African Mozambique and I could only be cheered to receive his gratitude, however little I had really done to deserve it. We warmly embraced in the middle of the hall.

I will repeat here the final passage in my speech to the United Nations that July 20:

"I appeal to the world, particularly to those countries which regard Portugal as an ally, which share arms and military training with it, which protect its interests at the United Nations, whose commercial companies pour money into the Cabora Bassa project only a very few miles from Wiriyamu—I appeal to those countries to think again, to realize that by continuing to do this, by closing their eyes to the genocidal policy of the Portuguese Government in Mozambique and elsewhere they have taken on their own hands the blood of the women and children of Wiriyamu. I call upon these nations to insist upon a full public and independent investigation of these charges, upon the bringing of Portuguese troops under proper control, upon the prevention of the use of NATO arms in Portuguese Africa—indeed, to recognize the profound and persistent wickedness of a whole course of policy which is at present being pursued and which has resulted only too predictably in the massacre of Wiriyamu."

•   •   •

There can be no possible question that a major massacre of villagers by the Portuguese army took place just south of Tete on December 16, 1972. The original report has been repeatedly confirmed from one side after another. It can still be asked whether these confirmations have all the same somehow affected the original picture. In particular they have all given lower figures. In August the Portuguese themselves admitted some fifty people killed at Chawola when 'contrary to standing orders isolated units did in one particular case at least commit reprehensible acts' (*Daily Telegraph*, August 20). On September 25 the Johannesburg *Star* claimed in a top front page article and editorial that it had obtained full confirmation from Portuguese sources for the shooting of a hundred people at Wiriyamu, among whom about twenty escaped. In October Frelimo declared in Dar es Salaam that its sources too report that some hundred people were killed in Wiriyamu, while other were massacred at Chawola but they do not at present know how many.

The original report which we published claimed that 'over four hundred people' had been murdered that day. I thought at the time that this referred to Wiriyamu alone, but it became clear when the Chawola report was published, and the version of the Wiriyamu report which Amnesty received was examined that the figure of over four hundred referred not to one village but to a wider area—a number of villages. It is only on this point that I would admit any inaccuracy in the report published on July 10. There is no reason to think that the total number of victims was fewer than four hundred.

It is curious how willing people are to accept a figure from the Johannesburg *Star* produced nine months after the event when not a single witness nor victim nor even journalist is mentioned by name, when they are unwilling to accept a figure established on the spot by named observers working within three weeks of the event and naming many of the victims and some of the survivors.

It is next to impossible for anybody—Frelimo or the press or even the Portuguese Government to establish months later the number of victims of a massacre of this sort, without a lengthy public inquiry. The survivors are now completely dispersed and few of them would voluntarily come forward. They are nearly all illiterate, speaking no language in common with most of the inquirers. Estimates of this distance of time are bound to be conjectural; if they come from the Portuguese side, they are likely to be minimising; and from wherever they come they are likely to relate to only one village whereas we know that there were in fact a number of massacres that afternoon. In fact the *Daily Telegraph* of August 20 exactly confirms the original report of fifty-three bodies at Chawola. The *Star* account, while speaking of Wiriyamu, still appears to be describing what happened at Chawola and not what happened at Wiriyamu. Its statement that the soldiers 'lined up the villagers, told them to clap their hands and, as they clapped, shot them down. Then poured petrol on the huts and bodies, set them alight, and left' exactly confirms what the original report of December 19 said of Chawola. As the Portuguese authorities interviewed Podista and other Chawola survivors in August (and could have done, of course, any time they wanted to from December on), it is fairly clear where the *Star* account in part first came from. Its admission from the Portuguese side that there was a massacre at Wiriyamu itself is none the less significant; but there is no reason to think that the figures it offers have great authority.

An inquiry by Frelimo at such a late date is also unlikely to reveal the full number of casualties, as they are very far from being in control of the area in question.

What we are left with is the original account of the Burgos Fathers. It has been confirmed on point after point: on the date, on both the main villages named, on the names of several of the survivors, on the number of bodies at Chawola, on the initial (apparently so improbable) 'bombing' of Wiriyamu. It was they who asserted from the start that all the Bishops of Mozambique had known about the massacre months before July and had protested to the Government and this has now been fully vindicated by the publication of the Bishops' statement of March 31.

At the end of it all we have a hundred and eighty names of victims compiled by the Fathers within three weeks and we have their assurance that the total number of the dead was more than double. That information was based on the fresh memory both of survivors and of soldiers who took part, was put in a report not intended for publication but precisely to enlighten a Portuguese bishop living on the spot who would naturally be quick to reject it if it contained exaggerations or unfounded charges by Spanish priests against his own government. Its whole character is such as to commend it. Since publication it has been confirmed in many things and disproved in none.

What has happened since? The journalists have come and gone. The DGS has stayed. The few survivors of Wiriyamu and Chawola as well as other people from the area have tried to find a new life in the *aldeamento* of Mphadwe, four kilometres from Tete, together with people from the villages of Guzinho, Kwiro, Nhautereze, Kapimbo, Nicombo and Malangwe. There little Domingos, the youngest survivor of Chawola, Antonio's brother, has died. Fifteen-year-old Antonio himself has got away, where to one does not know. Chico Kachavi, the DGS bully who urged on the killings on the spot, has been murdered with a grenade thrown into his house in Chimadzi on August 15. Whether it was the DGS or Frelimo, one does not know. He was never more than a convenient tool in the hands of his masters, but his elimination may now have appeared advisable. Colonel Videira, the military commandant in Tete who was certainly responsible for the action, has been dismissed from his post in September. A separate civil governor is again, it is said, to be appointed—some slight belated official response, not so much to the wickedness of what was done, as to the seriousness of the world's reaction. Fr Sangalo, one of the principal writers of the original report, has been expelled from Mozambique on August 24, 1973.

As to Wiriyamu itself it exists no more. And yet it will live for ever. Its name will be known as the name of no other village in the length and breadth of Africa: a symbol of defenceless humanity extinguished by genocidal tyranny.

Responsibility

Responsibility

WHO WAS responsible for the massacre at Wiriyamu? Clearly, the officers and men of the Sixth Commando Group who actually did the job; Chico Kachavi, the DGS agent who went with them to see that they did it really thoroughly and kept crying out 'Kill them all'; the senior officials of the DGS at Tete who had given the immediate orders; Colonel Videira, the military commander and governor of Tete, who was personally answerable for all major operations in the area.

But the responsibility did not stop there. Wiriyamu is not an isolated incident, it is part of a system and the expression of it, and it is those who have created and maintained the system who are responsible for its individual manifestations. Even in the line of massacres it does not stand on its own but as one of a long series of such incidents in both Mozambique and Angola, some of which we have heard (though never before in such detail as this) but most of which we have never heard: they were carried out too effectively and too far away from any mission or other channel to the outside world. But many Portuguese people themselves know only too well what has been done time and again, and it has been to get away from such atrocities that men like Major Ervedosa, formerly a staff officer in Angola, have deserted from the army and fled abroad.

The massacres altogether, however, are themselves only the last and most insensitive expression of a system of government whose whole character is brutal and destructive. At the end of it all massacre remains an exceptional event while forced labour, the compulsory resettlement of people in the concentration camp type locations called 'aldeamentos', the arbitrary arrest, interrogation and detention of suspects by the political police—all these are simply normal parts of the present Portuguese system. In particular it is essential to realise the true nature of the DGS, on which a very valuable statement was made at the UN Special Committee on Decolonization on August 2, 1973 by Niall MacDermot, Secretary-General of the International Commission of Jurists.

The power and evil reputation of the DGS, for long known as the PIDE, has been phenomenal for years. It has been a law unto itself and it is extremely improbable that Caetano himself either knows or can control most of what it is doing today. In Mozambique it is officially not answerable even to the Governor-General, but whether the government in Lisbon is informed of all its doings is quite another question. Great as its evil power has been for decades, it has grown of late both in theory and in fact. Decrees of July 18 and October 1, 1972 greatly increased its right to imprison and try people wholly within its own secret system. There is no judicial appeal or control of any sort possible. The police is to act against any person whom it considers has behaved 'contrary to the territorial integrity of the nation.' The whole normal administrative and judicial system is being simply left aside in the vast development of the DGS.

The system of government which exists in Portuguese Africa today is one which, while its defects are steadily increasing, is in essential continuity with the Portuguese colonial system of the past. It is a system which creates servitude. It is a cruel system. It is a facist system. It is a culturally destructive system. And it is a racist system.

It creates servitude by its use of forced and contract labour. The cornerstone of Portuguese colonial policy has been that the African must be forced to work. The abolition of slavery was consequently a relative one, expressed by Portugal's refusal to sign the Forced Labour Conventions of 1930 and 1946. A country in which trade unions are illegal, in which the vast majority of the population is illiterate, in which work is compulsory and in which special companies are licensed by the government to recruit men for European enterprises under a long-term contract to which they are then legally bound, is truly a servile one. This semi-slavery is taking a new form today through the development of the *aldeamentos.*

Its cruelty is symbolized by the *palmatorio*, the special wooden instrument used in the Portuguese colonies for beating people on the palms of the hands and soles of the feet. As Clifford Parsons, who was nineteen years a Baptist missionary in Angola, has written: 'The use of corporal punishment . . . has no one to question it in Angola. It is part of life, as everyone knows. The cheeky house-boy, the man who omitted to raise his hat to the *chefe de posto*, the clumsy labourer, the chief unable to produce the requisite number of 'volunteers' — all have savoured the *palmatorio* or the `chicote*. Doctors and nurses of our own missions have tended the hands of people beaten in this way. I myself have seen the backs of lads whipped in 1959 for no other reason than the suspicion that they might have been discussing politics' (*Angola; Views of a Revolt, OUP, 1962*, p.68). It is manifested in the day-in, day-out running of the political prisons and the tortures that go on there, tortures which brought Pastor Manganhela to his death. It is manifested by the massacre even of babies at Wiriyamu.

Its fascist character is revealed above all in the lack of all political freedom and in the ever-growing power of the DGS, the political police, a force modelled on the SS of Nazi Germany.

Its culturally destructive character is the other side of its primary aim of 'Portugalization.' It does not allow Africans to be themselves, to have a culture and a language that matter. The purpose of government and the very condition for such citizenship as is open to black people is psychological identification with Portugal. This policy is quite simply one of cultural genocide. Indeed it is clearly because the non-Portuguese Protestant missions could hardly identify with such an aim, rather than because of their religious character, that they have always been under such suspicion from the government: As a policy paper at a special government symposium on 'counter-subversion' held in Angola in 1968 declared: The Protestant missions, being 'under heavy foreign influence,' work 'contrary to the Portugalization of the native masses.' (Jose de Figueiredo Fernandes, paper dated September 25, 1968).

Finally, the system is racist. This is often denied. Indeed defenders of Portugal go to great lengths in affirming the non-racist character of its rule. It is therefore particularly necessary to be clear upon this point. It is not legally racist in the sense that it provides a clear differentiation in law for people of different races. It does not do so. The Portuguese have always accepted social mixing between the races and the establishment of a racially mixed group more or less tied to the service of, and some participation in, white society. This is a decidedly good quality in the Portuguese colonial tradition. It was, of course, closely related to the very small number of Portuguese and their vital need to associate with themselves some native groups. Unlike South Africans, they have always been willing to put arms into the hands of native soldiers.

Yet, apart from the odd individual who has totally identified himself with Portugal, there has been a very clear limit to the height that such people could rise. Power remains always in white hands, even more so now than in the past. General Kaulza de Arriaga has declared the maintenance of 'white supremacy' to be 'a national objective' (Lectures on strategy given at the Institute for Higher Military Studies, 1966-7). In Mozambique the white population is far less than 5% of the whole. How can such an objective not result in gross discrimination against the black 97%? And of course it does all the time. Every black man who comes into any prominence and is not an absolute stooge of the government will be at once under suspicion and is likely quickly to find his way to Machava detention camp as a possible threat to that 'national objective' and probably to the 'territorial integrity of the nation.' That is why Domingos Arouca, the first black Mozambican doctor of law, has been in prison and detention for over eight years charged with 'psychological subversion.' That is why Fr Pinto de Andrade, the best-known black Angolan Catholic priest, has been in prison and detention since May 1960. That is why hundreds of pastors and leaders of the Protestant Churches were arrested in June 1972. Their very existence is a challenge to that 'national objective.' White lawyers and priests are not treated in the same way. They may be arrested and harshly used, but they don't just disappear without trial as blacks certainly do.

Let us listen to the words of Bishop Felix Niza Ribeiro of Joao Belo, speaking on oath as a witness in court at the trial of Frs Sampaio and Mendes in Beira, February 1972. He declared that racialism was simply a part of the way of life of Mozambique: 'Do you want an example of what I have stated? Together with these two priests a black man was accused of the same crime and imprisoned on the same day. Where is he now? Has he lawyers to defend him? What happened to him and, above all, why? Because he is black.' (from the transcript of the trial.) The man in question was a simple mission servant, Joao Chabuca. He was arrested on even slighter charges than the two priests—who were finally given very minor sentences by the court and immediately released — but he completely disappeared, despite all the inquiries of lawyers. That is what happens to most black men who are arrested by the DGS. There is no legal racialism but the practical racialism is still worse.

The present Portuguese system of government in Africa is creative of servitude, cruel, fascist, culturally destructive and racist. It is that whole system which is symbolized by Wiriyamu. And the responsibility for it lies not with the local officials in Tete but with the heads of the police and the army, the leaders of the state itself and Marcello Caetano most of all. The tardy removal of the Commander in Tete—who may have been less involved than the top officers in the DGS there — in no way exonerates Caetano from his own basic responsibility for this and many other atrocities all of which are part of the system he has inherited and maintained, and to which his own personality imparts a certain civilian and academic respectability.

Is Frelimo responsible? Surely such massacres would not take place if there was no war, no violent liberation movement? Has not Frelimo created the situation in which such things happen and must therefore bear the blame for what happens as a result? Moreover, if the Portuguese commit atrocities, does not Frelimo commit even bigger ones? It is not the purpose of this book to analyze the nature of Frelimo, its organization or capacity for victory in the war. What is important to remember, however, is first that Frelimo represents a movement of revolt of the people of Mozambique themselves. It is not engineered from outside, although it is of course helped from outside. Its basic support comes from people in every part of Mozambique. The violence and injustice which have long formed an integral part of the Portuguese colonial system, together with Portugal's refusal to envisage any non-Portuguese future for these territories make it inevitable that more and more Africans should choose the course of violent resistance. The violence of the system has produced, and is responsible for, the violence of the revolution. If you are a complete pacifist you will not, even so, believe such a course a right one for the oppressed. If you are not a complete pacifist, it is difficult to find any sound ground for condemnation. There are many European pacifists and Christian pacifists, but neither Europe nor Christianity has been significantly pacifist for centuries. One thing that Christians in Europe cannot do is to impose upon African Christians pacifist standards which they have never practised themselves.

What about the massacres perpetrated by Frelimo? Frankly, I do not believe in them. And I will not do so on the authority of Portuguese communiqués, any more than I would believe in Portuguese massacres solely on the authority of Frelimo communiqués: both are too interested parties and Portuguese communiqués have been shown to be totally unreliable time and again. I have asked many missionaries, including Portuguese people, who have worked actually in the war areas whether they knew of such massacres. Each one of them has replied in the negative: that they know cases of Frelimo having killed local chiefs or other individuals who have collaborated with the Portuguese, but they know of no cases of indiscriminate murder by Frelimo. In Dortmund in September 1972, I was asked to take part in an open debate on the question of Portuguese Africa with Herr Kühl, a Protestant pastor who is sympathetic to the Portuguese position, lived in Lisbon for some years and had only just returned from several weeks in Mozambique. He frankly admitted that the Portuguese had committed massacres but claimed that Frelimo had carried out even bigger ones. However, when I asked on what authority he said this, whether any missionary working in the war areas had said that this was so and that he had evidence of it, Herr Kühl was forced to admit that it was only people in Lourenco Marques and Beira who said they thought Frelimo had committed such atrocities. Despite his strong assertions and recent weeks in Mozambique, he had no worthwhile independent evidence to offer whatsoever. From this I conclude that tales of such massacres are a Portuguese fabrication.

If Portugal is directly responsible for these atrocities, it is not alone in this responsibility. It shares it with those powers who are bolstering up, and profiting from, Portuguese rule in Africa. Those powers are South Africa and Rhodesia, and behind them many forces in western capitalism. In many post offices in Mozambique today you can see a poster depicting the three flags of Portugal, South Africa and Rhodesia with the motto 'United we stand.' This expresses the reality. Rhodesian troops have frequently been operating inside Mozambique and South African troops are guarding the Cabora Bassa dam, whose chief function will be to provide power for the Transvaal. More and more western European, especially German, investment is going into Portuguese Africa, and the greater part of the military equipment used by the Portuguese comes from Germany. In permitting the continuance of this monstrous trade Willy Brandt is, curious as it may seem, showing himself to be a successor to Adolf Hitler—insofar as he is effectively supporting the régime which more than any other today carries on the Nazi tradition, and at the expense of Africa. He is, of course, inheriting a policy of the Christian Democrats and one protective of the interests of German capitalism. In continuing it, he may have a greater effective responsibility for the maintenance of Portuguese tyranny in Africa today than any other man. It was with reason that Frelimo recently rejected the offer of minor financial assistance from the German Social Democratic party.

Western capitalism as a whole is, however, responsible for what is happening. It is its wealth which has been channelled through consortia based on Johannesburg to build Cabora Bassa, some fifty miles away from Wiriyamu. Western interest in Mozambique is not, however, only related to what it actually invests in that country: it is much more concerned to maintain the Portuguese presence as protection for South Africa. South Africa is the western world's ideal investment area: the political situation there, producing the appallingly low wage scales for Africans, has made it so. The presence of Portuguese Africa eliminates any possibility of an external threat to South Africa and its continuance is, as a consequence, of the greatest importance both to South Africa and to its investors elsewhere. Whether the war goes on indefinitely or not, what happens to the people of Mozambique, how many young Portuguese die or are maimed in the struggle, how Portugal is itself brought to ruin — none of this matters very much, so long as a certain military and police presence is maintained to keep black rule from approaching South Africa.

All these are the powers which are responsible for Wiriyamu —powers which are oppressing Mozambique. The Portuguese people are not responsible for Wiriyamu. On the contrary, they are intimidated and silenced by the DGS and the whole system of Caetano's government, just as the people of Mozambique and Angola are.

It was the voice of Chico that shouted 'Kill them all!', but the powers that paid him, that provided the weapons, that needed his services were not only the DGS, General Kaulza de Arriaga and Marcello Caetano, but the producers of military equipment in France, Germany and Britain, the governments of John Vorster and Ian Smith, the economic empire of Anglo-American. It is with all of them that responsibility lies.

Where does the Church stand?

Where does the Church stand?

THE GREAT majority of Christians in Mozambique are Roman Catholics. The Protestant missions in the country were always small; it was never easy for them to work in a Portuguese territory. We have seen something of the present plight of some of these churches. The Catholic Church, however, is in a different position. It is large, closely connected with the government and very influential. We have now to consider its position inside the Mozambique conflict of today.

It can never be easy to minister within a situation of civil war. But when the Church is so closely tied to a government hated by the majority of people as much as that of Mozambique is today, the situation does indeed become next to impossible. And some priests have found it so, yet others struggle on for so long as they are allowed. What is striking is how many have now come out in the strongest protest despite the gag which the Concordat was calculated to impose. Of many of these priests we have hardly heard—of Fr Cecilio Regoli, for instance, an Italian member of the Consolata Fathers, summarily expelled in November 1970; of numerous Portuguese priests who have been quietly hurried back to Lisbon. If we add together the White Fathers, the Burgos Fathers, the Portuguese seculars of the Beira diocese and others who have either been expelled or prevented from returning to Mozambique after leave, we come in all to a figure not far short of a hundred: 20% or more of all the white priests in the country.

It is clear enough that these missionaries of today have realised the intrinsic relationship between proclaiming the Gospel and working for a just society and have drawn consequences in Mozambique unacceptable for the government.

Nor have the bishops been entirely silent. Only the Archbishop of Lourenco Marques has really attempted a defence of the government's position. All the others appear more or less unhappy with it. We have seen their protest in March 1973 over Wiriyamu. Bishop Sebastian de Resende of Beira was well-known for his defence of the rights of Africans and several others have protested, at times openly, more often privately at this or that injustice. The present bishop of Nampula, Mgr Manuel Pinto, has done more than this, taking on much of the mantle of de Resende in a still more difficult time. His disagreement with government policy is well-known and it was he who told Fr Da Costa to go abroad: 'Talk, denounce, tell the world what is happening here!'

After the departure of the White Fathers in 1971, the expulsion of Mgr Duarte de Almeida and the resignation of Bishop Cabral, Mgr Pinto of Nampula was appointed temporarily as administrator of Beira diocese. While there, he and the remaining priests in the diocese drew up and signed a statement deeply regretting the attacks that many had made upon the White Fathers: 'We are sorry . . . that people have not understood that the attacks on the missionaries were, and are, attacks on the missionary Church in Mozambique. And so it seems to us that this is the moment when the Church in Mozambique . . . should seriously think about the reasons which made the White Fathers abandon the mission stations of Beira and Tete . . . The confusion which occasionally shows itself in the relations between the State and the Church raises questions which we cannot ignore. We want to see the Church in Mozambique more independent and autonomous in its own sphere . . . we prefer a Church that is persecuted but alive to a Church that is generously subsidised but at the price of a damaging connivance at the behaviour of the temporal powers.'

For the most part it must be said, however, that the bishops of Mozambique have not spoken out, have not taken up any position which could seriously embarrass the government and have therefore not truly proclaimed the Gospel within this situation. One reason why they have not done so is only too clear: they are paid by the government, their appointments depended upon government approval, they have to send in regular reports about the Church to the government. They are mostly good men but placed in an impossible situation. Their work has been absorbed into that of the government to such a degree that independent public action becomes almost unthinkable. All this is so because of the Concordat and Missionary Agreement made between the Pope and the government of Portugal in 1940. In return for very considerable financial help, a privileged position and permission to introduce some non-Portuguese missionaries into Portuguese Africa, the Catholic Church surrendered its freedom of action, merged its work with that of colonization and blessed the official Portuguese view of what missionary activity is meant to be.

That view we have seen already. The Catholic missions are 'instruments of civilization and national influence,' (Colonial Act, 1930), 'institutions of imperial utility' (Missionary Statute, 1941), and effective tools of Portugalization. It is of the utmost importance that the real thrust of the *Missionary Agreement* should be clearly understood. That is why it has been included in full in an appendix together with sections of the *Concordat* and the *Missionary Statute*. The aim was to make of the Church a tool for 'Portugalization.' It would be incredible were it not true that at the beginning of the charges in the indictment of Frs Valverde and Hernandez, it is stated that 'As foreign missionaries in the service of Portugal they received their relevant subsidies and other benefits attributed by the statute, and in exchange agreed to convert their flocks to the Portuguese way of life'. Here lies without ambiguity the basic Portuguese understanding of what the Catholic Church has agreed to do by the *Missionary Agreement* and what men like Valverde and Hernandez must be punished for failing to do.

It is not only foreign missionaries who have found this a monstrous caricature of what they are trying to do. More and more Portuguese too have risen against it—men like the twenty-six priests and twenty-nine seminarians of the Portuguese province of the Society of the Holy Ghost (which has big responsibilities in Angola though none in Mozambique) who wrote in 1968 to protest against the whole official missionary mystique

as it had been fed to them: 'The Portuguese missionary follows
the road of his ideal: to carry Christ to the world and to tell men
what Portugal is.' Such an approach, they declared, was out-of-
date and ridiculous. Not only ridiculous but extremely harmful,
and yet it is a view of mission somehow countenanced and
justified by the agreement made between Rome and Lisbon.

More and more the Church in Mozambique is torn apart between fidelity to the Gospel and fidelity to the Concordat. And if
the Church in Mozambique is thus torn, is not the Church in
Rome torn too? The Pope spoke out about Northern Ireland,
about Biafra, naming them, but he has not done the same for
Mozambique, even though Catholic priests are there faced with
a situation of far clearer injustice than could be found, all in all,
in those other two places. He is tied by the Concordat to diplomacy instead of to a clear message expressive of truth and justice
for a society in agony.

The Missionary Agreement is not wrong merely because the
government with which it was made is now acting in a grossly
tyrannical manner. It is of the greatest importance to remember
that it is wrong for still more basic reasons which hold even if
the government were far more gentle and humane. It is wrong,
first, because it implies an unacceptable view of mission, as something which can be linked with and made to serve colonial assimilation, the destruction of African culture.

It is wrong, secondly, because in accepting a position of privilege, almost 'establishment' for the Catholic Church in Portuguese Africa, it implies that the Catholic Church is in fact the
majority Church in Angola and Mozambique—which it is not.
The great majority of the inhabitants are not Christians. The
Missionary Agreement involves carrying the privileged position
of the Catholic Church in Portugal, where it is indeed the Church
of the vast majority of the population, into other lands where it
is not.

Thirdly, it is wrong because by giving privileges to Catholics,
it discriminates against Protestants. Thus it divides Christians,
embitters relations between them, and puts Protestants into a
civilly underprivileged position—and this with the clear conniv-

ance of the authorities in the Catholic Church.

Fourthly, it is wrong because it puts the Church effectively into bondage. The more dependent it is financially upon the government, the more unable it is to proclaim its message freely and fearlessly. The government is even allowed to veto senior appointments to ensure that its leadership will remain subservient; although in several cases—all credit to the bishops—this has not worked: most notably of all in the case in Portugal itself of the present Bishop of Oporto, Dom Antonio Gomes Ferreira, who was for long exiled by Salazar.

Fifthly and finally, the Concordat system becomes further disgraceful when—as at present—the government is in fact behaving in an extremely tyrannical and oppressive manner. The same men who are authorizing massacres and torture are paying the bishops' salaries and travel tickets, and receiving their annual reports.

The missiological significance of the withdrawal of the White Fathers in 1971 has not, it seems, been sufficiently pondered by the Catholic Church. It is probable that the White Fathers constitute the most professional group of missionaries it possesses. They are certainly not a highly politicized group of priests, indeed their rules instruct them to avoid politics. Their withdrawal after very careful thought from a position in which they were not prevented from baptizing or distributing the sacraments and in which they had more financial assistance than they receive in any other part of Africa, constitutes an affirmation of immense importance as to what Christian mission in the nineteen seventies should be primarily about. By an immensely hard decision, involving the ending of the particular work to which thirty or forty men had given themselves for years and in which they had intended to continue for many more, they were saying something about mission, about the message of salvation for our time, about the Church's priorities, which the central authority of the Church does not appear to have heard. It was perhaps much the same message which came from the Bangkok Conference sponsored by the World Council of Churches in January 1973. If Rome had taken the action of the White Fathers with full seriousness, it might not have been caught quite so unprepared for the crisis precipitated by the imprisonment and expulsion of the Burgos Fathers and the publication of the report of Wiriyamu. Its tools of concordat and diplomacy are essentially inadequate, indeed wrong, to cope with a situation of this kind. It is time and more than time that this church-state alliance, created by the Concordat and the Missionary Agreement, should be terminated.

It is time for the sake of the missionaries on the spot betrayed by it into a position of impossible ambiguity. It is time for the sake of the people of Mozambique and Angola that they be offered a true Mission, a true Church, a true Gospel, not an article officially tied to 'Portugalization' by 'instruments of national influence.' It is time for the sake of the Church, Christian and Catholic, everywhere that she be no more dishonoured, tied by such dubious arrangements to the perpetrators of cultural genocide and massacre. It is the integrity of the Gospel which is at stake, together with the human honour of those who have committed themselves to its proclamation.

In the words of an appeal to Pope Paul signed by 700 people at the twenty-first Conference of Christian Studies at Assisi in October 1973: 'The Catholic Church has adopted a position of grave compromise and co-responsibility: for the alliance over the centuries between evangelization and colonization, for its adhesion to Portuguese colonial power, consolidated with the stipulation of the concordat, for complicity in destruction of local culture, for the identification of the Christian message with western culture, for the lack of support, for intimidating and repressive action, even, against members of religious orders who have had the courage to denounce such crimes to public opinion, for the guilty ambiguity in the rare and mild initiatives in favour of the oppressed populations, for still not having uttered any explicit condemnation of colonial exploitation and war.'

Canon Burgess Carr, the Secretary General of the All Africa Conference of Churches, appealed to Pope Paul in December 1972 to abrogate the Concordat. The regional conference of the Mary-knoll Sisters in Africa in January 1973 supported this appeal, as has Archbishop Milingo of Zambia. Canon Burgess Carr subsequently visited Rome to urge the matter in person. On September 26 the Executive Committee of the All Africa Conference of Churches not only repeated this appeal to the Pope but also urged the Conference of all Catholic bishops in Africa to take up the matter and even the Organization of African Unity to ask its member states to review their relations with the Holy See 'in the light of its collaboration with Portuguese repression in Africa.' Increasingly Rome's insistence upon maintaining an evangelically and theologically indefensible position for diplomatic and financial reasons is going to involve it in an ecumenical and international debâcle of vast proportions. Maintenance of the Concordat is coming to be seen for what it truly is—a betrayal of the Gospel. The Church cannot bring tyrannies to an end and there are many tyrannies in the world besides that of Portugal, but it can and must refuse to be party to them. If it does not do so, if it prefers the crumbs and bus tickets of the tyrant to being a credible 'sign of salvation' in a suffering world—can it still truly be called the Church of Christ? If it can, it is not because of but despite the Secretariat of State and the diplomatic rôle of Rome. It is because of Valverde and Hernandez in their prison cells in Machava and all those like them who proclaim the freedom of God's future through their commitment to liberation in the present.

The road to Jericho

The road to Jericho

The Church has not merely to free herself from the charge of collaboration with oppression and injustice, and then to withdraw from the area of conflict into some haven of the purely spiritual. She has to be herself a credible community of freedom and of liberation. The message that she proclaims and the life she endeavours already to live is a life of freedom—freedom not only of the spirit but of the whole man. In Mozambique as everywhere in the world, if the Church is to be the true Church, it must challenge oppression and enhance the sphere of freedom. That is the basic affirmation of Da Costa, Valverde, Hernandez and those who think, work and suffer with them. It was with such thoughts in mind that in the autumn of 1972 I preached the following sermon in the Reinold Kirche in Dortmund.

*   *   *

'I have come that men may have life and may have it in all its fullness' (John 10.10).

Jesus Christ came to give life, more abundant life. But what does this more abundant life mean? and if he came to bring life, to what are Christians committed? The abundant life that Jesus Christ claimed to bring was the life of the Kingdom of God— a Kingdom that was both to come in the future and was clearly present: the Kingdom of God is among you. It is a Kingdom that exists by the light of God's truth, and by the power of God's love—a truth and a love manifested in Christ and communicated by him to mankind. This truth and this love are the inner core of the abundant life Christ has pledged himself to give us — a

life which transforms and revivifies the half-dead life of the
world. It revivifies this world life all through, starting with that
which is most manifest: The lack of life in the very limbs of
man. To the paralysed man Jesus says — 'Stand up, take your
bed' (Mt 9.6). It is at this most physical level that the liberating
life of Jesus is first manifested: Here is the sign, the sacrament,
of the new life of the Kingdom:

'Jesus went round the towns and villages, announcing the good
news of the Kingdom, and curing every kind of disease and ail-
ment'. (Mt 9.35.) Always these two things go together and must
go together: the proclamation, the *Kerygma* — and the service
of man's here and now secular need, the *Diakonia*.

Jesus summarized his work in these great words: 'Go and tell
John what you hear and see: the blind recover their sight, the
lame walk, the lepers are clean, the deaf hear, the dead are raised
to life, the poor are hearing the good news' (Mt 11. 4-5).

Jesus is the sacrament of the new and fuller life. By the message
he speaks he sketches it out; by his behaviour and the life of the
company centred around him, he is its visible manifestation and
inauguration; by his secular concern, his compassion with the
here-and-now needs of mankind around him, he authenticates it
—even the smallest needs he is bothered about, going so far as
to defend and justify his companions satisfying a small feeling of
emptiness in the stomach by plucking and eating some ears of
corn as they walked through the cornfield on a Sabbath Day.

This pattern of an integrally and intrinsically combined *Kerygma*
cum *Diakonia,* he bequeathes to his disciples: to be as he has
been—the sacrament of the Kingdom not only by their proclaiming that Jesus is the Christ but by the strength and quality of
their human concern. Indeed it is in this human concern that the
Kingdom will be found and entered into: 'Enter and possess the
Kingdom, for you gave food, you gave drink, you took me into
your house, you clothed me, in prison you visited me' (Mt 25. 34-6).

The provision of food, drink, hospitality and clothing are not
a definitive list of secular concern, but are simply its most obvious
and primary exemplars. Nor do they only concern man's needs in
relation to purely physical forces; 'in prison you visited me'—here

already is the indication of the still vaster diakonia of liberation not from purely physical conditions, but in and from the consequences of man's own treatment of man.

Of all this Christians, and the Church which is the body of Christians, are and must be the continual sacrament and embodiment: by their immediate relevant service in the world of their day pointing towards, and making credible, the coming of the Kingdom. Without that service, the gospel of the Kingdom is not credible, and not authentic, and not realised in the flesh as the true word of God must be. Word made flesh, word in flesh—the flesh of Christ responding to the flesh of the leper, the paralytic, the Samaritan. The flesh of Christ is the sacrament of life, but only because it exists in a world of flesh, and has its immediate message to offer to that world: a liberation which is of this world first, as was the original exodus liberation, and across a this-worldly liberation—physical, psychological, social and political—pointing to the ultimate fulness of liberation in God and with God.

The first disciples knew instinctively that their task was the same: to give what they could in response to a secular need as the sign of the Messiah's coming and glorification.

Generally the response would be of a simple kind, occasionally of a striking one: Think of Peter and John faced with the paralysed man at the gate of the temple; 'I have no silver and gold; but what I have I give you: in the name of Jesus Christ of Nazareth, walk' (Acts 3.6). What a storm this caused. If Peter and John had kept to the 'religious' sphere, if they had limited themselves to praying in the temple for the poor man, there would have been no such storm. But they gave what they had in response to real human need. They demonstrated the secular power of the gospel within the order of this world and for that—the proclamation of a resurrection of Jesus which could overturn things here and now—they were arrested and brought on trial before 'the rulers of the people and the elders' (Acts 4.9).

A gospel which is not related, not earthed, in the over-turning of the secular, the liberation of this worldly man, is indeed the opium of the people, the 'Sugar-Candy Mountain' of George

Orwell's *Animal Farm*. And 'the rulers of the people' are glad indeed that the Church, the sons of the apostles, should provide the people with opium—with the promise of a liberation in the next world which is a tranquilliser and a substitute for liberation in this one.

Here is the unavoidable contrast and conflict between religion which is opium and religion which is a sharing in the life of the word in the flesh: one substitutes a liberation in the next world for freedom and a better life in this one, the other finds liberation in the next world in and through a liberation here and now, which is essentially a total human response to all the needs of our fellow men. This last and this alone is the authentic mission of the Gospel, the *Kerygma* enfleshed in *Diakonia*, the word incarnate in the secular service of man: our neighbour.

My friends, this service is as old as the Gospel, but in our day it is taking and must take forms adapted and significant for our world and our contemporaries. Who is my neighbour? Jesus was asked. You will find him on the road to Jericho, he replied. The road to Jericho is always there but each age finds it in a different place. Where today is our neighbour? Where today the man who has fallen among thieves? Where today the priest and the levite— the bishops, the devout religious people—who have passed by on the other side? He is in many places, but I can tell you one of them.

It is southern Africa—in the Republic of South Africa, in Mozambique, Angola and Rhodesia. Here is a part of the world where over 35 million Africans are held in various degrees of racial servitude by some four million white people: they are so held by political, legal, economic and social discrimination and by a brutal and ruthless police and army. They are so held in order that their white masters should enjoy a greater affluence than any other society in the world, and that the myths of racialism— of white superiority, of Portugal's civilizing mission, of the identification of so-called Christian civilization with the rule of the white man—should be maintained. But they are not only held in bondage by and for the white people of southern Africa; they are also held by and for the people of Western Europe, and in particular Britain, France and Western Germany. We Europeans are both keeping in existence and profiting from this monstrous racialist and fascist tyranny. We do it by the sale of military equipment, the vast economic investment, the continual sharing of technological know-how. While Western Europe continues to invest millions in Cabora Bassa and similar projects throughout southern Africa, while it continues to sell military equipment to Portugal, it is involved in, and in a major manner responsible for, and identified with, these tyrannies. I do not need to remind you that they are, in a very close historical manner, the extension and continuation of Nazism; that the Nationalist Party of South Africa was strongly influenced in its formative years by the Nazi Party, and the DGS/PIDE, the immensely powerful secret police of Portugal, was modelled quite explicitly upon the German SS.

If hundreds of women and children were slaughtered last December at Wiriyamu and Chawola, only a few miles away from Cabora Bassa, if eleven miners were shot only last September by the South African Police in Johannesburg, if the political prisons of Machava and Robbins Island are fully of detainees, if many are tortured, if wages are desperately low, malnutrition and infant mortality extremely high within a land of affluence—you and I, as members of the society of western Europe, which is collectively supporting South Africa and Portugal, are responsible. Here for us is a road to Jericho; here for us is the man sitting paralysed at the gate of the temple; here for us is the Christ hungry, homeless, in prison; here for us is entry to the Kingdom, the *Locus* for diakonia, the this worldly sacrament for our time in which can become incarnate the liberation of the gospel, the more abundant life proclaimed by Jesus.

Refuse it we easily may: the priest and the scribe have already done so. The 'rulers of the people' have already denounced the liberation of a cripple. We can join the priest and the scribe and the rulers of the people very comfortably. We can continue to sell our military equipment to Portugal, to invest our money in Cabora Bassa, to say that all this is not our affair: we did not personally strike the blow that knocked down the man upon the road to Jericho. Let us pass on the other side of the road. We can

do so, my friends, and we shall go together to hell, into the judgment of those who, rejecting their neighbour, reject Christ and
the life he has brought, however many times we still cry 'Lord,
Lord'. The right and the left, the sheep and the goats, the priests
and the Samaritan: did you tend my wounds or did you not?

'I have come that men may have life and may have it in all its
fulness.'

Appendix 1

Appendix 1

The Concordat

(An agreement between the Portuguese Republic and the Holy See, signed May 7, 1940).

Article I

The Portuguese Republic recognizes the personality in law of the Catholic Church.

Friendly relations with the Holy See shall be maintained in the traditional, historical manner by the appointment of an Apostolic Nuncio to the Portuguese Republic and of a Portuguese Ambassador to the Vatican.

Article XXVI

The ecclesiastical division of the Portuguese Overseas Dominions shall take the form of dioceses and self-governing missionary districts. Missionary boards may be set up within both by the respective prelates, by agreement with Government.

The boundaries of the dioceses and missionary districts shall be fixed so as to correspond as far as possible to administrative divisions.

Article XXVII

Religious life and missionary apostolate in the diocese shall be ensured by the respective residential bishop and, in the missionary districts, by the missionary corporations.

The recognized missionary corporations shall establish in Portugal or on the Neighbouring Islands training establishments and rest homes for their missionary staff. The establishments and homes of each corporation shall form a single institution and will be subsidized from the Central State Budget.

Missionary dioceses and districts, other ecclesiastical bodies, religious institutions which may be established in Portugal or on the Neighbouring Islands, shall be acknowledged to possess personality in law. Missionary dioceses and districts shall be subsidized by the state.

Article XXVIII

When a sufficient number of Portuguese missionaries is not available, the Ordinaries of the missionary dioceses and districts may, by agreement with the Holy See and with the Government, call in foreign missionaries who shall be incorporated in the missions of the Portuguese missionary organization, provided they declare themselves to be subject to the laws and courts of Portugal, on terms suitable to ecclesiastics.

Whenever in each missionary diocese or district new missionary boards are established, the appointment of the respective Directors, when the individuals selected are not Portuguese, can only be made after consultation with the Portuguese Government.

All missionaries whether national or foreign, belonging to the secular clergy or to religious corporations, shall be entirely subject to the ordinary jurisdiction of the prelates of the missionary dioceses and districts, insofar as missionary work is concerned.

II
Missionary Agreement between Portugal and the Holy See

Bearing in mind:

That on this day the Concordat between the Holy See and Portugal has been signed;

That in the Concordat arts. XXVI to XXVIII contain the fundamental provisions relating to missionary activity;

That during the negotiations for the signing of a Concordat the Portuguese Government proposed that these provisions should be later expanded into a private Convention;

The Holy See and the Portuguese Government have decided to stipulate an agreement to regulate more completely the relations between the Church and the State are far as religious life in the Portuguese overseas territories is concerned, all that has been previously laid down for the Patronage of the East to be observed without alteration.

For this purpose Plenipotentiaries have been appointed, to wit: His Eminence the Most Reverend Cardinal Luigi Maglione, Secretary of State to His Holiness, for the Holy See; and HSE General Eduardo Augusto Marques, formerly Minister of the Colonies, Chairman of the Corporative Chamber, Grand-Cross of the Military Orders of Christ, of S. Bento de Aviz, and of the Order of the Colonial Empire; HE Dr. Mario de Figueiredo, former Minister of Justice and Religion, Professor and Director of the Faculty of Law in the University of Coimbra, Member of Parliament, Grand-Cross of the Military Order of Santiago da Espada; HE Dr. Vasco Francisco Caetano de Quevedo, Envoy Extraordinary and Minister Plenipotentiary to the Holy See, Grand-Cross of the Military Order of Christ and Knight of the Order of S. Gregorio Magno, for Portugal; who have agreed on the following provisions, under the reserve of ratification;

Art. 1

The ecclesiastical division of the Portuguese Colonies will be made into dioceses and autonomous missionary districts.

It is the task of the Bishops of the dioceses to organize the religious life and work of apostleship of their own dioceses through the secular and regular clergy.

In missionary districts religious life and the work of apostleship will be the onus of missionary corporations recognized by the Government. This does not mean that missionaries of other corporations or the secular clergy may not work in those territories, when so authorized by the Government.

Art. 2

When there is not a sufficient number of Portuguese missionaries, the Ordinaries of the dioceses and missionary districts may, in agreement with the Holy See and the Government, call on foreign missionaries, who will be admitted to the missions of the Portuguese missionary organization once they have declared their submission to Portuguese laws and courts. This submission will be such as is suitable for ecclesiastics.

Art. 3

The dioceses will be governed by residential bishops and the missionary districts by Apostolic Vicars or Prefects, all being of Portuguese nationality.

In both, the Catholic missionaries of the secular clergy or of religious corporations, whether Portuguese or foreign, will be completely subject to the ordinary jurisdiction of the prelates mentioned above, insofar as missionary work is concerned.

Art. 4

The dioceses and missionary districts will be represented vis-à-vis the Government of Portugal by the respective prelate or by his delegate, and the missionary corporations by its Superior or by his delegate.

The Superiors and delegates herein mentioned shall be of Portuguese nationality.

Art. 5

Recognized missionary corporations shall establish in European Portugal or on the neighbouring islands training and rest establishments for their missionary staffs.

The training and rest establishments of each corporation constitute a single institute.

Art. 6

Three dioceses are hereby created in Angola, with their seat at Luanda, Nova Lisboa and Silva Porto; three in Mozambique, at Lourenco Marques, Beira and Nampula; one in Timor, at Dili. Furthermore, missionary districts may be set up in those colonies, and also in Portuguese Guinea.

By agreement with the Portuguese Government, the Holy See

may alter the number of dioceses and missionary districts. The limits of the dioceses and missionary districts will be fixed by the Holy See so as to correspond, as far as possible, to the administrative division, and must always fall within the limits of Portuguese territory.

Art. 7

Before proceeding to the appointment of a residential bishop or a coadjutor *cum jure successionis,* the Holy See shall communicate the name of the person chosen to the Portuguese Government, in order to know whether there are any objections of a general political nature to be brought against him. The absence of any reply from the Government within thirty days after the communication has been made will be taken to mean that there are no such objections. All the consultations provided for in this article will be confidential and secret.

Whenever new missionary centres are set up within each diocese or missionary district, and where the appointment of the respective directors does not fall on Portuguese citizens, it can only be made after the Portuguese Government's opinion has been sought.

When an ecclesiastical district is created, or when it becomes vacant, the Holy See may at once appoint a provisional apostolic administrator, before proceeding to make a permanent appointment. The appointment of such administrators shall be communicated to the Portuguese Government.

Art. 8

The juridical personality is recognized of dioceses and missionary districts, other ecclesiastical bodies and the religious institutes of the colonies, and also of the male and female missionary institutes set up in European Portugal or on the neighbouring islands.

Art. 9

Recognized missionary corporations, male and female, will be subsidized according to needs by the Government of Portugal and the Government of the respective colony, independently of the help they receive from the Holy See. In the distribution of such subsidies, account will be taken not only of the number of students in the training establishments and the number of missionaries in the colonies, but also of the missionary works, including therein seminaries and other works for native clergy. In the distribution of the subsidies which are the liability of the colonies, the dioceses will be considered on equal terms with the missionary districts.

Art. 10

Apart from the subsidies referred to in the previous article, the Government will continue to grant land free of charge, when available, to Catholic missions for their development and new foundations. For the same purpose the bodies mentioned in article 8 may receive private subsidies and accept legacies, bequests and donations.

Art. 11

The following shall be exempted from any kind of tax or levy, both in Portugal and in the colonies,

(a) All the goods and property which the bodies referred to in article 8 possess in the pursuance of their aims;

(b) All the acts *inter vivos* of acquisition or relinquishment, effected by the bodies named for the achievement of their ends, as well as all the provisions *mortis causa* in their favour for the same ends.

Moreover, sacred images and other objects of worship shall be free from all customs duties.

Art. 12

Apart from the subsidies provided for in article 9, the Portuguese Government guarantees the residential Bishops, as the Superiors of the missions of the dioceses concerned, and the Apostolic Vicars and Prefects, payment of suitable stipends, and will maintain their right to receive a retirement pension. For journeys or movement, however, they will have no right to any displacement allowance.

Art. 13

The Portuguese Government will continue to pay the retirement pension to retired missionary staff and in future it will pay it to the members of the missionary secular clergy when they have completed the requisite number of years of service for this purpose.

Art. 14

All missionary staff will be entitled to reimbursement of travel expenses within and outside the colonies. To enjoy this right, it is necessary only for the Ordinary or his delegate to present to the Government in Portugal a list of the names of the persons, together with a medical certificate testifying to the necessary physical stamina for life in the Overseas territories. No other formalities are necessary. If the Government has reason to consider the medical certificate insufficient, then it may order a new examination to be carried out by trustworthy doctors. Lady doctors shall always be provided for female missionary staffs.

Return journeys to Portugal because of health reasons or for the enjoyment of leave will be authorized according to the standards laid down for civil servants, on the application of the respective prelates.

Art. 15

The Portuguese Catholic missions may freely expand in order to exercise the forms of activity proper to them, especially the foundation and direction of schools for natives and Europeans, colleges for boys and girls, institutions of elementary, secondary and technical education, seminaries, catechism schools, ambulances and hospitals.

In agreement with the local ecclesiastical authority, Portuguese missionaries may be entrusted with the services of religious assistance in schools for Portuguese nationals in foreign territories.

Art. 16

In missionary schools for natives tuition in the Portuguese language is obligatory but, in harmony with the principles of the Church, the use of the vernacular in the teaching of the Catholic religion is quite untrammelled.

Art. 17

Since Ordinaries, missionaries, auxiliary staff and missionary nuns are not civil servants, they are not subject to the disciplinary regulations or any other provisions or formalities to which civil servants may be subject.

Art. 18

The Prelates of the dioceses and missionary districts and the superiors of the missionary corporations in Portugal shall furnish the Government annually with information on the missionary movement and external activity of the missions.

Art. 19

The Holy See will continue to use its authority so that the Portuguese missionary corporations may intensify the evangelization of the natives and missionary apostleship.

Art. 20

The Parochial regime of the diocese of Cabo Verde remains in force.

Art. 21

The two texts of the present Agreement, in Portuguese and in Italian, shall have equal force.

Vatican City, May 7, 1940

III

The Missionary Statute Decree-Law No 31,207 April 5, 1941
[A law of the Portuguese Republic implementing the Agreement with the Vatican of the previous year]

Art. 1

The Catholic Church in the overseas territories is guaranteed the free exercise of its authority. Within the sphere of its competence it possesses the faculty of exercising its powers of order and jurisdiction without any hindrance.

For this purpose the Holy See may freely publish any provision relating to the Government of the Church and communicate and correspond with the Prelates, Clergy and Catholics in the overseas territories on all that refers to its pastoral ministry, as may the latter with the Holy See, without the necessity for any previous authorization of the State for bulls and any instructions or decisions of the Holy See to be published and have currency within overseas territories.

On the same terms, this faculty is conceded to the Ordinaries and other ecclesiastical authorities with reference to their clergy and flock.

Art. 2

The Portuguese Catholic missions are ecclesiastical organizations recognised by the Government in the terms of the Concordat and the Missionary Agreement.

The Portuguese Catholic missions are considered to be institutions of imperial utility and to possess an eminently civilizing sense.

Art. 3

The Portuguese Catholic missions may freely expand in order to carry on the kind of activity proper to them, especially to found and direct schools for natives and Europeans, colleges for males and for females, institutes of elementary, secondary and technical education, seminaries, catechism schools, ambulances and hospitals, in the terms of this decree-law.

Art. 4

The ecclesiastical division of the colonies will be into dioceses and autonomous missionary districts. Missionary centres may be created in either.

Art. 5

The creation of dioceses and missionary districts is effected by the Holy See which can, by agreement with the Government, alter the number of dioceses and missionary districts.

The limits of the dioceses and missionary districts will be fixed by the Holy See in such a way as to correspond as far as possible to the administrative division of the overseas territories, and always within the limits of Portuguese territory.

Art. 6

Missionary centres will be set up, in agreement with the Government, by the Prelates of the area in which they will carry out their activities.

Their limits will be fixed so as to correspond wherever possible to administrative divisions.

Art. 7

When a Prelate desires to set up a missionary centre, he shall inform the Ministry of the Colonies of his intention, through the governor of the colony, with an indication of the reasons motivating it.

The Minister of the Colonies will give his reply in the shortest possible space of time.

Art. 8

The dioceses and missionary districts will be recognized to possess a juridical personality, as will other ecclesiastical bodies and the religious institutes of the colonies, which are thus held to be moral persons with juridical capacity.

The dioceses and missionary districts will be legally represented by their Ordinaries. The other moral persons will be represented by their Ordinaries or by the latter's delegate.

Art. 9

The dioceses will be governed by resident Bishops, and the missionary districts by Vicars or Apostolic Prefects.

The residential Bishops and the Vicars or Apostolic Prefects shall always be Portuguese nationals.

Art. 10

The missionary centres will be governed by directors, who may be simple priests.

The Superiors of missionary centres, when not Portuguese, may only be appointed after the Portuguese Government's opinion has been sought.

Art. 11

In the dioceses religious life and apostleship shall be guaranteed by the Bishops through the secular or regular clergy, European or native.

Art. 12

In the missionary districts religious life and apostleship shall be guaranteed by missionary corporations recognised by the Government.

Art. 13

By missionary staffs are meant the following only: the Prelates and their secular clergy and the members of the male and female missionary corporations who, according to the precepts of their institutes, dedicate themselves to the work of apostleship in the colonies.

Art. 14

Missionaries are those priests who, in complete subordination to the Prelates, devote themselves exclusively in the colonies to the diffusion of the Catholic faith and the civilizing of the native population, and auxiliaries are those who, while not priests, co-operate with them to attain the same ends, to which they devote themselves absolutely.

Art. 15

In principle the missionary staff shall be of Portuguese nationality. The Ordinaries of the diocese and the missionary districts may, however, call upon foreign female missionaries or missionary staff when this is clearly necessary to make good a lack of female missionaries or missionary staff of Portuguese nationality.

1. Before calling upon foreign missionaries, the Ordinaries must first obtain the express agreement of the Portuguese Government and the Holy See. Residence in the colony will not be permitted to those who have not been so called upon by the Ordinaries or who have been called in contravention of the provisions of this paragraph.

2. Foreign missionaries will always form part of the missions of the Portuguese missionary organization.

Art. 16

The foreigners referred to in the second part of the previous article will only be allowed to enter Portuguese overseas territories when they have expressly declared that they renounce the laws and courts of their nationality of origin and submit to the laws and courts of Portugal, which will henceforth be the only ones empowered to rule and judge them. This declaration does not relate to the subordination of the missionaries to canon law, the legitimate ecclesiastical authorities and the tribunals of that nature.

Sole. The declaration to which this article refers will be made in duplicate on ordinary paper, directed to the Minister of the Colonies and written and signed in the declarant's own hand before a notary, who will testify to this on the documents themselves.

A copy of the declaration will be placed in the archives of the Ministry of Colonies and the other will be sent by the Ministry to the governor of the colony to which the declarant is going.

Art. 17

The Government will refuse its consent to the calling in of any foreign missionary who does not prove his ability to speak and write the Portuguese language fluently.

Art. 18

As far as misionary work is concerned, missionaries, whether of the secular clergy or the regular clergy, will be entirely subject to the ordinary jurisdiction of their Prelates, according to canon law.

Art. 19

In those colonies having a governor-general the Bishops will receive a stipend, equal to the salary of a governor of a province which is not that where the capital of the colony is situated, from the budget of the colony where they exercise their spiritual jurisdiction. In other colonies, the Bishops will receive a stipend equal to the salary of the best paid head of a service. The Archbishops of the archdioceses of Luanda and Lourenco Marques will receive stipends equal to the salary of the governors of the provinces of Luanda and Lourenco Marques respectively. Those Prelates who are not Bishops will receive a stipend equal to the salary of the directors of services of the civil administration, or to that of heads of services of the civil administration, according as they exercise spiritual jurisdiction in colonies having a governor-general or in simple colonies. If, however, any Prelate should be appointed Apostolic Administrator, he may not accumulate the stipend due to the Ordinary of the ecclesiastical division he administers with the stipend due to him in his capacity as Bishop, Vicar or Apostolic Prefect.

Art. 20

The Prelates are not entitled to a displacement allowance when they travel, but they will be reimbursed their travelling expenses. To obtain this reimbursement, they shall apply to the Minister of the Colonies, when in Portugal, or to the governor of the colony, when in the overseas colonies.

Art. 21

When any diocesan Bishop, Vicar or Apostolic Prefect wishes to absent himself from the colony he shall previously inform the governor of his intention to do so and shall indicate, whenever possible, for how long he will probably be absent. When he is temporarily or permanently substituted in the government under his jurisdiction he shall indicate the name of the person appointed to substitute him. Where the Bishop, Vicar or Apostolic Prefect concerned cannot make this declaration in person, it will be done by his substitute.

Whenever any director of a mission has to absent himself from the area of the diocese or missionary district concerned, or is replaced as director of the mission, the Bishop, Vicar or Apostolic Prefect to whom the mission is subordinated shall make the communication or indication to which the first part of this article refers, which may be addressed to the governor of the respective province.

Art. 22

The resignation or transfer to Portugal of any Prelate entitles him to receive a retirement pension, if he has served the requisite number of years in the overseas territories for this to be granted.

The Prelate concerned shall apply for this pension to the Minister of the Colonies.

Art. 28

Priests will travel first-class and other missionary staff second. Within the colony nuns will be entitled to travel first-class.

Art. 43

The missionary institutes will be subsidized according to needs by the Government of Portugal.

Art. 44

The distribution of subsidies to the missionary institutes needing them will be effected as follows:

Half of the overall sum included in the budget of the Ministry of the Colonies for subsidizing the missionary institutes will be divided equally among all the institutes. The other half will be distributed in proportion to the number of students in the training establishments of each institute destined for mission work and the number of missionaries for which the institute is responsible who have returned from the colonies as being unfit for further service, due to illness or old age.

Art. 47

Sums will be included in the colonial estimates to subsidize dioceses and missionary districts. These sums will be distributed by the government of the colony, taking into account the number of missionaries working in each diocese or missionary district and the missionary works existing there, including seminaries and other works for native clergy.

The Prelates will distribute the sums received as they think fit.

Art. 66

Teaching especially intended for natives shall be entirely in charge of missionary staff and auxiliaries.

The Governors will come to an agreement with the Prelates of the diocese and missionary districts on the transfer of native education from the services of the state to those of the missions, and shall publish such Orders as are necessary to regulate this transfer.

Sole. In places where missions have still not been established or where they are unable to exercise at once the functions entrusted to them by this article, native education will continue to be the responsibility of the State, but only until the missions are able to take over this work.

Art. 67

The governors shall regulate by Order the holding of final examinations for those natives who have attended the native teaching schools of the missions for award of the respective diploma and will grant it the validity which is considered to be suitable.

Art. 68

Native education will obey the policy laid down by the Political Constitution, will be considered for all purposes official and will be regulated by the plans and syllabuses adopted by the governments of the colonies.

Those plans and syllabuses will aim at the perfect nationalization and moralization of the natives and the acquisition of habits and skills of work, according to the sexes, conditions and conveniences of regional economies, such moralization to include the abandonment of sloth and the training of future rural workers and craftsmen who can produce enough for their needs and social liabilities.

Native education will thus be essentially nationalist and practical, conducive to the native's being able to obtain means for the maintenance of himself and his family, and will take into account the social state and the psychology of the populations for whom it is intended.

It will be the task of the government, through the education services of the colony concerned, to indicate what technical knowledge is most suitable for teaching to the natives.

Art. 69

In schools the teaching and use of the Portuguese language is compulsory. Outside the schools the missionaries and auxiliaries will also use Portuguese.

For the teaching of religion the native tongue may be used without restriction.

Art. 77

Within the first ninety days of each year the Prelates of the dioceses and missionary districts shall send a detailed report on the missionary work effected during the year to which the report refers to the governor of the colony in which they exercise their spiritual jurisdiction.

This report shall indicate the staff employed in each mission, showing the respective classes and sexes and the number of foreigners, by class and sex, and their nationality.

It shall also indicate the changes in staff that occurred during the year, clearly showing new staff, those who have returned to the staff after leave and absent staff, all divided according to class and sex.

All indications as to staff shall mention the corporation to which they belong.

This report shall also show the total expenditure on salaries and personal bonuses and will show the distribution of the State subsidies among the various missions or missionary establishments.

The Prelates' reports are considered sufficient justification for the subsidies received from the colonies.

Art. 78

The Superiors of recognized missionary corporations shall send to the Minister of the colonies, within the first one hundred and twenty days of each year, a detailed report on the missionary activities of the missions entrusted to the members of their corporations.

The Superiors' reports are considered to be sufficient justification for the subsidies received from Portugal.

Art. 79

The missionary corporations and institutes are not State bodies or departments.

Art. 80

The missionary staff and auxiliaries are not civil servants, nor are they subject to the disciplinary regulation or other provisions or formalities to which civil servants may be subject. They are considered as staff engaged on a special service of utility to the nation and civilization. They only enjoy the benefits granted by this decree so long as they are exercising their ministry or when they return to Portugal, having fully satisfied the condition for payment of a life pension, if they are entitled to such and with due authorization.

Art. 81

The European or native staff engaged on native education, including teachers, are not civil servants.

Art. 82

The Authorities and public services shall give all the help and support, in the exercise of their functions, that the development and progress of Catholic missionary action necessitates, in harmony with their national and civilizing aim.

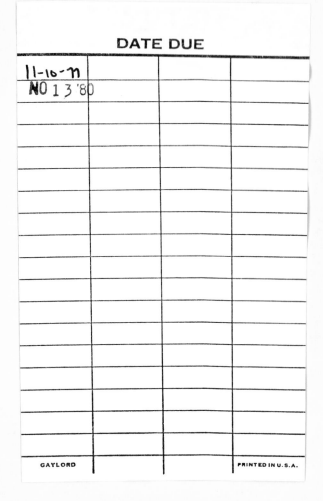

DATE DUE

11-10-77			
NO 13 '80			
GAYLORD			PRINTED IN U.S.A.